FOREWORD

The purpose of this book is to provide a comprehensive and easy-to-use guide for visitors to one of San Diego's most precious open space jewels, Mission Trails Regional Park. Mission Trails is one of the largest natural urban parks in the country. It offers a varied combination of facilities, educational opportunities and recreational programs rarely found in other cities. Some visitors come seeking a quiet area for repose and reflection; others play a round of golf, cheer on a Little League team, fish for trout at Lake Murray or sleep under the stars at Kumeyaay Lake Campground. Hikers, bicyclists and horseback riders use the many trails. And the inquisitive learn about the history of the people who lived here centuries ago at the Park's state-of-the-art Visitor and Interpretive Center.

San Diego's Mission Trails Regional Park: Official Guidebook is a collaborative endeavor of the Mission Trails Regional Park Foundation, park staff, and volunteers. The book was created under the guidance of local writer Pamela Crooks, who also authored *Discover Balboa Park: A Complete Guide to America's Greatest Urban Park*. Its publication would not have been possible without the generosity of the underwriters, SDG&E Sempra Energy Utility, San Diego Landfill Systems, and City of San Diego Special Promotional Programs.

Park patrons will find this guide to be a welcome addition to our visitors' services enhancements. Keep a copy in your backpack, enjoy, and visit often.

Dick Murphy
Mayor
City of San Diego
August 7, 2003

San Diego's

MISSION TRAILS
REGIONAL PARK
OFFICIAL GUIDEBOOK

by
Pamela Crooks

with contributions by
Ruth Alter
Clark Rasmussen

Illustrations by
Sue Carlton Sifton

Mission Trails Regional Park Foundation

Ridgway Park Publishing
La Mesa, CA

First Edition

Editorial Consultant: Donald E. Steele
Layout & Production: C & L's, www.clparts.com
Printing: Partner Press, El Cajon, CA

Library of Congress Catalog Card Number:
2003095295

ISBN 0-9706219-1-4

Write to us: Mission Trails Regional Park Foundation
One Father Junipera Serra Trail, San Diego, CA 92119
www.mtrp.org

E-mail: mtrp@mtrp.org
or
editor@ridgwaypark.com

Table of Contents

CHAPTER **5**

What to See & Do ...73

Five Regions: Descriptions & Trail Info ...74

CHAPTER 6

Special Opportunities in MTRP   ...121

APPENDIX

COAST LIVE OAK

CHAPTER 1

Mission Trails Regional Park – An Unfolding Legacy

On a rainy day in February, I sit inside my hilltop aerie overlooking the craggy cliffs and mist-shrouded peaks that tower over Middle Earth... Am I dreaming? Have I just seen the latest film version of Tolkien's famous trilogy?

No. I'm enjoying the inspiring view from the reference library at the Visitor and Interpretive Center at Mission Trails Regional Park on a stormy day. Kwaay Paay (Kumeyaay words for "The Chieftan"), one of the most impressive peaks framing my view, is a popular rock climbing site in the Park, reached by following the

Climbers Loop Trail that winds through an area affectionately known as "Middle Earth" by climbers.

The trail is one of the shorter ones among a system of hiking, biking and equestrian paths that would measure over 40 miles if stretched end to end. The library I'm using is a great resource for anyone interested in the natural history of the Southern California/Baja, Mexico region. One can find not only an array of technical books on everything from astronomy to geology, and field guides to the plants and animals of the area, but also light reading on a variety of subjects ranging from American Indian stories to environmental topics. There are also many wonderful children's books relating to nature and the environment.

In 1996, retired SDSU librarian and Park volunteer, Muriel Standeven-Foster described the role of the Visitor Center and its library. "The Visitor Center is a frame for the Park; the form of the education is experiential. The library is an important contributor to the education..."

This is just one of the gems I gleaned during a day researching the historical archives of the Park's non-profit foundation. Just one, among the hundreds of stories of land being acquired, sewage pipes rerouted, sensitive habitat reclaimed and replanted with native plants, trails being cleared, fences built, historical artifacts protected, bridges and signage installed, funds raised and Trails Guides trained.

Besides progress updates on the parkwide trail system, a staging area for Cowles Mountain and the building of the magnificent Visitor Center and Kumeyaay Lake Campground facilities, there were also inspiring stories of lives enhanced and changed by Mission Trails, plant, animal and insect lore, tips on bird watching, safety, fishing, hiking and stargazing.

One theme consistently running through all the information I reviewed, is the ongoing spirit of cooperation and partnership among the citizens, their elected officials and public employees. This public/private partnership continued even as the players changed over the last few decades. This in itself is a remarkable story.

One person who was around in the early days of planning a park at the eastern edges of San Diego was Pauline des Granges, Director of the Park and Recreation Department for the City from 1964 to 1974. She credits most of the early vision to city planning staff. They were looking at general plans of the City at that time and saw areas where they might potentially be able to acquire land for the City to save it from development.

Two other factors were important in the creation of MTRP. Much of the land within the Park was not developed earlier because it was held by the utilities department (water) from the late 1920s in case it was needed in the future for dam purposes. The area also served as an important watershed for decades. Not until 1954 could the land be used for a purpose other than watershed, according to Pauline.

Much of the area—including all of one mountain, the stream bed and the Old Mission Dam—had been part of the original Mission Tract of land conveyed by the Spanish government to the Church and later to a patron of the Mexican government and his descendants. This, as well as some U.S. government land in Santee, managed by the Bureau of Land Management, was acquired by the City around this time.

"A plan was then developed in the late 1950s or early 60s—perhaps to keep the land from being sold," says the former Park and Recreation Director. Today we call this concept "open space" planning.

"The first plan developed for this park (MTRP) was not too different from the current plan, except there was more emphasis on active recreation for the community," she continued.

"Since that time, whenever subdivisions are designed, plans for open space and parks have to be included, as we see in Scripps Ranch and Tierrasanta."

She feels the private citizens who served on Park and Recreation committees, working tirelessly on the master planning of these communities with city planning staff, deserve much of the credit.

This kind of vision and tireless work by unsung community leaders has also been essential to the development of one of the largest open space urban parks in the nation. One such leader is Dorothy Leonard, who as chair of the Navajo Community Planners in 1974, saw an opportunity to preserve some of the last undeveloped land in her neighborhood for future generations to enjoy. When Jim Ellis, a friend and City Councilmember for District 7 at the time, overheard talk of development moving forward on Cowles Mountain, he consulted with Dorothy. They decided to explore whether it was feasible for the City to buy the land. Jim put together the legislation, which was unanimously approved by City Council. However, the deal required a $2.2 million loan and approval by the County Board of Supervisors.

Jim approached Dick Brown, his counterpart on the Board of Supervisors representing the 2nd District, who agreed to at least take a look at the potential purchase— from the air. His district included the county-owned Gillespie Field in El Cajon.

Even though that flight took place almost 30 years ago, Dorothy, Jim and Dick will never forget the view they had flying over the lands that would one day be included in Mission Trails Regional Park. As they flew west and north over Cowles Mountain, Mission Gorge, Fortuna Mountain and the San Diego River making its way to the ocean, they could see new housing being built in almost every direction, with the exception of these pieces. The trip really opened their eyes to the possibilities.

"We <u>have</u> to save this land!" they all agreed.

With the assistance of city and county staff who provided the needed background research, Dick convinced two of his fellow supervisors to support his motion to help the City purchase the Cowles Mountain parcel, just in time to meet the deadline of the developer—midnight on December 31, 1974. Despite heated opposition, the deal passed on a vote of 3-2 around 8:30 p.m.

More land acquisition followed, especially after approval by the voters of Proposition C in 1978, which authorized $65 million in bonds to be sold to buy open space. The rest, as they say, is history.

When asked why San Diego is blessed with not one, but three great urban parks—Balboa Park, Mission Bay Park and now Mission Trails Regional Park—Pauline des Granges explained that the incorporated area of San Diego far exceeds most other cities, making it possible to have these large parks.

"Eastern cities are much more confined and compact. We've had space through the years. Our early history played a role. Pueblo (city) lots granted by the Spanish king to the new community of San Diego were very large. These and other Spanish land grants created huge tracts of land in California which affected the way our cities later developed."

Certainly this has been an important factor; but without the vision, commitment and partnership of public employees, elected officials and long-term community volunteers, the treatment of these large tracts might have turned out very differently.

For more detailed information, including a chronology of the Park's development read the first chapter of this book, especially "A Park Is Born."

A successful public/private partnership continues today, and will continue for the foreseeable future. The Park is administered by the City of San Diego Park and Recreation Department under the leadership of Director Ellen Oppenheim, with oversight by an intergovernmental agency known as the Mission Trails Regional Park Task Force, which includes six elected officials, one each from Santee, and La Mesa, two from the City of San Diego, and two members of the County Board of Supervisors. The chair of the MTRP Citizens' Advisory Committee (an advisory committee to the Task Force made up of concerned people who represent cities and community groups adjacent to the Park) is also a member of the Task Force.

A non-profit public benefit organization [501(C) (3)] known as the Mission Trails Regional Park Foundation has an agreement with the City of San Diego to co-manage the Visitor and Interpretive Center and other Park facilities. Through a volunteer board this Foundation also raises funds for projects identified in the original Master Plan, and to enhance and promote the Park

The non-profit MTRP Foundation, the fund-raising and advocacy arm for the Park, meets monthly. Grants for the Foundation's programs are often funded by the City Council with funds generated from Transient Occupancy Tax (hotel room tax). Similar grants have been received from private foundations and donations from corporations and other private parties. The Foundation's most important function is to educate the public about the importance of maintaining and preserving this precious resource for many generations to come. City staff and Foundation volunteers work together daily toward this important goal in Mission Trails Regional Park. (PC)

CHAPTER 2

Mission Trails Regional Park –
A River Runs Through It

OLD MISSION DAM

San Diego ranks as the seventh largest city in the United States with almost 2 million in population. Blessed with one of the greatest climates in the world, interesting topography, beaches less than a half-day's drive from mountains and deserts, and its proximity to Mexico, it is no wonder that so many people want to live, work, vacation or retire here.

As a recent immigrant to the area idles in a rush hour traffic jam on Interstate 8, one might wonder what the region was like before it became so populated. Surrounded by futuristic freeway overpasses, glass-fronted office buildings, shopping malls and numerous hotel properties, it's hard to imagine Mission Valley as the peaceful place it once was, intersected by a lazy river making its way to the ocean. Or to picture Kumeyaay villages dotting the green, verdant areas along the river.

But one does not have to travel more than about 10 minutes away from this rush hour scene on Interstate 8 to be transported to another place and time. Mission Trails Regional Park, one of the country's largest urban open space parks, lies just northeast of I-8 where the San Diego River passes through a rugged area known as Mission Gorge...

Long before there were ever humans inhabiting the region, the river was carving out a pathway to the sea. With origins high in the Cuyamaca Mountains, fed by winter snow melt and natural springs, the river grew as it made its way down steep hillsides – always pulled by gravity, always finding the route of least resistance. It probably began traveling this way when the area lay much closer to the equator, in a time before coastal California began moving northward along the San Andreas Fault. The air was humid, rainfall was constant and vegetation lush. The first mountains in this region were volcanic in nature, forming a range called the Santiago Peaks.

The mountains people climb in Mission Trails Park today were not formed until much later, as pressure and heat below the earth's mantle, where one continental plate collided and submerged under another, fused igneous material with sedimentary rock and thrust huge granitic formations to the surface. As the second ice age ended, water from melting glaciers and ice caps further north caused the Pacific Ocean to rise and move inland as far east as the Cuyamacas where ocean fossils can be found today.

As the ocean retreated from the sharp granite peaks in Mission Gorge, wind and water continued to shape the landscape. The rainfall became more seasonal, with river flows ranging from steady to torrential in the spring. Geological evidence tells us that Mission Valley itself was formed when a huge river spanned the entire width we see today. As recently as 1916, the valley floor was once again covered by the usually quiescent San Diego River.

But generally speaking, for the last 10,000 years the climate has been similar to the semi-arid climate we know today; the San Diego River has traveled the same route through the rocky gorge and scenic valley beyond, only occasionally overflowing its banks on its way to the Pacific.

Earliest Inhabitants

(From here to the end of this chapter Archaeologist Ruth Alter made significant contributions.)

According to archaeologists, humans began to appear in the region about 10,000 years ago. The earliest documented residents were the San Dieguito people (named for a river in northern San Diego County) who were present in San Diego from about 8000 B.C.E. to about 3000 B.C.E.

Another group known as the La Jollan culture was present in San Diego from about 3000 B.C.E. to about 1 C.E. Only a trace of San Dieguito presence and only a few La Jollan sites can be found in Mission Trails Regional Park today.

The Kumeyaay Period

It's no surprise that this fertile area would later become home to a sizeable band of American Indians known as the Kumeyaay. In fact, the area we know today as MTRP, and its surrounding areas, would have provided a vast variety of materials for food, medicine, tools, clothing and shelter. Acorns and grass seeds were gathered to be pounded into meal. Tule reeds, willow, and juncus found along the San Diego River became rafts or house thatching, bark skirts for women and girls, and coiled or twined baskets.

Flat granite rocks become kitchen grinding surfaces and quartz was fashioned into projectile points to tip arrows. Even the clay dug from along the banks of the river would have been fashioned into pottery storage jars, cooking pots or bowls. Whatever resources were present in the Park found their way into knowing Kumeyaay hands.

As long as 1,000 years ago, the Kumeyaay began occupying the village they called "Senyaweche," a large portion of which is located beneath what is now the Carlton Oaks Golf Course and housing tracts in Santee. Occupants of Senyaweche are believed to have been part of the labor force conscripted by the Mission padres to construct the Old Mission Dam in the early 1800s.

The village endured well into the historic period, with its inhabitants finally dispersing between 1900 and 1910, after the land was purchased by American ranchers and farmers. A few Kumeyaay remained even after this period, working as ranch or farm hands. Today, tribal jurisdiction for the area is claimed by the Viejas band of Kumeyaay.

EWAA

To the Kumeyaay, the land itself and all its features and resources were powerful living entities. People were part of the natural world; in exchange for receiving the benefits that the land, plants and animals provided, people had certain responsibilities toward them. The land had to be kept clean, which meant burning off the understory of the oaks each year; large game animals had to be killed respectfully, which entailed following prescribed rituals; and in particular, water courses were specially cared for, with banks and river beds kept free of debris.

The Kumeyaay were the first people to extensively live within and make use of the lands that became part of Mission Trails Regional Park. Traditional Kumeyaay villages were arranged in a dispersed pattern. Unlike European villages where houses were frequently clustered together, Kumeyaay families preferred living further apart. Often brothers would establish houses near one another or their parents, although no set pattern was strictly followed. Some of the sites found in Mission Trails Regional Parks represent Kumeyaay living areas.

The Spanish Period (1769-1822)

In 1769, a small band of Spanish Catholic missionaries and their soldier escorts from Mexico, reached what is now San Diego. Led by Father Junipero Serra, a Franciscan priest, their job was to establish the first of a series of missions in Alta California, intended to bring Christianity to the native people. Serra selected the first mission site on a promontory above the San Diego River, overlooking the Kumeyaay village of "Cosoy."

But in 1774, Serra moved the mission to a new site roughly six miles upriver, near the Kumeyaay village of "Nipaguay." The new mission was named Mission San Diego de Alcala.

Spain granted the Church vast areas of land for the Mission's use. This tract included 58,875 acres and extended from the pueblo land boundary of San Diego inland to the El Cajon Valley and from National City to Clairemont.

Soon after arriving in San Diego, Serra sent scouting parties up the San Diego River to look for suitable dam and basin sites. Mission Gorge was identified as an ideal location, but ample resources, including labor, weren't available at the time. It wasn't until about 1809 that work would begin. Using Indian labor from the Mission population and, presumably, the villages along the river, including Senyaweche, dam construction was undertaken.

While all of the California missions had some sort of water delivery system, the dam and flume constructed for the Mission San Diego de Alcala was by far the most ambitious. Built across the head of Mission Gorge, the 244-foot long, 13-foot thick, 13-foot wide dam was constructed of stone and cement on exposed bedrock, creating a permanent reservoir behind it. Water was released through gates and spillways into a gravity fed tile-lined flume, down the gorge and into Mission Valley, ending in a settling basin near the Mission.

Construction was completed by 1815 and the padres finally had a dependable source of irrigation water for their crops. A recent discovery at the Old Mission Dam suggests that the padres also used the pent up power of the dam to turn a grist mill for grinding corn and wheat flour—important staples in their diet.

Following completion of the dam, a largely prosperous period ensued at the Mission for the next 15 years. But after the secularization of the missions in 1833, the dam and flume were not maintained. Flume tiles were viewed as choice roofing materials and were carried off to be used in the homes of the pioneers. Later floods, particularly the flood of 1916, washed away much of the flume.

The Mexican Period

Over the years the secular population living behind the Spanish Presidio's protective stockade grew. Around 1820, with ties to Mexico about to be cut by a revolution, the citizens of San Diego slowly left the now crowded Presidio, moved down the hill, and founded the pueblo of San Diego in the area we know today as Old Town.

When Mexico won its independence from Spain in 1822, the citizens of San Diego had mixed feelings. Under Spanish rule, the people of the pueblo shared common lands for grazing and raising crops, while the richest land was held by the Church. All this now changed with a series of decrees that divided up the former Spanish lands and ultimately wrested the mission lands from the padres, creating enormous tracts of privately owned property.

But for the missionized Indians, the process of secularization was devastating. Most drifted away, until in 1842 only 500 remained at the Mission San Diego de Alcala; two years later the number had dropped to 100. The Mission was unable to support them and was also unable to pay the salary of its final majordomo, Santiago Arguello, who had been trusted with overseeing its remaining resources.

By 1845, the Mexican territory was facing the threat of American invasion. The Mexican president issued a proclamation directing the officers of the state to prepare to defend themselves. He vested them with extraordinary powers in order to use all means necessary. Under this order, the last Mexican governor of Alta California, Pio Pico, sold most of the missions to raise the money needed to finance the defense of Mexican holdings.

Governor Pico "sold" the San Diego Mission, its cattle, and its lands, including what is now Mission Trails Regional Park, to San Diegan Santiago Arguello, a patron of the government in Mexico City who had served in various political and military offices in San Diego. The deed for the transaction was drawn in Los Angeles in June, 1846.

Arguello never lived on the former mission lands; he made his home at Rancho Tijuana. His ownership of the ex-mission lands, however, was honored. In September, 1876, long after his death, Arguello's heirs were issued an American government patent declaring them owners of the tract.

The American Period

California's wealth had been noticed by the United States. By 1842, U.S. Navy ships were regularly cruising offshore, and by 1845 Americans were openly expounding the idea of a United States that stretched "from sea to shining sea." Within two years, after a series of battles, Mexican California came to an end and the United States laid claim to the territory. By 1850, California became a state and joined the Union.

During this period, the land in and around MTRP came under a variety of new uses, as well as new owners. Ranching, farming, mining, recreation, and military activi-

ties were initiated, but much of the land remained undeveloped. In 1885, the former mission lands were opened
up for settlement and a number of ranches and farms were
purchased in the area. One of the most notable tracts was
Rancho Fanita, owned by the Scripps family; dairy farming was represented by the Edgemoor Dairy. Beans were
regularly planted for years between Cowles Mountain and
Lake Murray.

Mining in Mission Gorge

Beginning in 1873, granite mines appeared in Mission
Gorge. Light gray in color, the granodioritic rock extracted
from these mines was used to construct roads, buildings,
jetties, and dams. Blocks of granite from the Gorge were
used in the construction of a breakwater in San Diego Bay
and are still in place today.

Modern mining industries, which provide sand,
gravel, and decomposed granite products, evolved out of
the early granite mining business. Many firms extracted
sand and gravel on lands that are now part of Mission
Trails Regional Park. In addition, the Morse Construction
Company operated a dynamite magazine on park premises
in the 1960s. Kumeyaay Lake and other nearby ponds are
the by-products of these mining operations, created by the
removal of rock materials.

Water Issues

As San Diego grew, the need for a reliable water
source became as critical to the City Fathers as it once had

been to the Mission padres. By 1920, the location of a new dam on the San Diego River was being debated.

Two powerful San Diegans, Colonel Ed Fletcher, owner of the Cuyamaca Water Company, which held title to a mile and a half of the San Diego River, and wealthy magnate John D. Spreckels, each championed different sides of the debate. Fletcher wanted to sell his water interests to the City for $1.4 million and argued that the best place for a new dam was below the Old Mission Dam, on land he owned. Spreckels, represented by the City Attorney, was outraged, claiming that the City already held all of the river's water rights as established under Spanish law, which subsequently passed to Mexico and then to the United States. They argued for an upriver location, at El Capitan.

In 1924, in a special election, citizens voted down a bond measure to construct the dam in Mission Gorge, but later that year approved a bond issue to construct the dam at El Capitan by a three-to-one margin.

In 1930, a second bond measure was put before the voters, who were once again asked to fund the construction of a dam one-half mile below the old Mission Dam. It too failed, and this time by an even greater margin than the first. In 1934 El Capitan dam was finally built.

Although Col. Fletcher eventually lost the battle for his preferred location of a dam further west on the San Diego River, he and his partner in the Cuyamaca Water Company, James Murray, were involved in the creation of another important dam. Its origins date back to 1895, when the San Diego Flume Company built a small, earthen and rock-paved structure to dam up a small creek running through Alvarado Canyon. It was called the La Mesa Dam.

For almost two years after a major flood in 1916 destroyed or damaged several other area dams, the water behind the La Mesa Dam served as San Diego's only water supply. As a result, the Cuyamaca Water Company decided to build a larger structure, and constructed a multiple arch concrete dam, 117 feet tall and 870 feet long, just downstream of the La Mesa Dam. This new, larger dam was dedicated in 1918 and named for James Murray, a water resources entrepreneur and Fletcher's partner in the Cuyamaca Water Company.

In 1926, the company sold its holdings to a publicly held irrigation trust in East County, which became Helix Water District; in 1961 this group granted ownership of Murray Dam and its reservoir, better known as Lake Murray, to the City of San Diego.

If a larger dam had been built anywhere in Mission Gorge in the 1920s or 30s, large portions of the land that became MTRP would have disappeared beneath its waters.

Military Uses

The military presence in Mission Trails Regional Park dates back to 1917, when U.S. Army personnel based at Camp Kearny a few miles to the west, used Fortuna Mountain as an artillery target as part of World War I training exercises. This practice was repeated when the area was reactivated as a military base in 1934, this time as Camp Elliott, a U.S. Marine Corps training center.

Ordnance was fired at the mountain for the next ten years, when the land was turned over to the U.S. Navy. The lands around Fortuna Mountain were used for infantry, tank and artillery training during World War II and the Korean War.

In 1960, about one-third of Camp Elliot's lands were declared excess holdings and were transferred to the General Services Administration. Between 1960 and 1963, some of this property was given to the City of San Diego, San Diego State University, and the San Diego Unified School District. Ultimately much of this land became part of MTRP.

Unexploded ordnance was an unfortunate legacy of the military period. Hikers sometimes discovered unexploded materials along the trails, especially after rainy periods, and it became clear the ordnance posed a serious public safety hazard. In 1993, an intensive sweep of the area was conducted and tons of unexploded materials were removed.

A Park is Born

In the 1960s, the Navajo Community Planning Area, which includes what is now MTRP, began to experience a major housing boom. As new developments sprang up everywhere, the City of San Diego decided an urban park was needed and explored the possibility of setting aside 1,765 acres of open space that included Fortuna Mountain, Mission Gorge and Old Mission Dam.

In 1967, with no City park yet in the works, the County of San Diego prepared its own regional park plan. This plan called for creating two smaller parks: Fortuna

Mountain and Lake Murray. By 1972, a new County plan called for linking the Lake Murray recreational area to the open space on Cowles Mountain. But no action was taken on this plan either, and housing tracts continued to be constructed at an overwhelming pace.

In 1974, Cowles Mountain was in imminent danger of being developed when an opportunity to buy it suddenly arose. This purchase laid the cornerstone for the Park the citizens of San Diego enjoy today and forged the inter-governmental cooperation needed to help make the Park a reality. (See pp. 12-13 for more details of the aquisition.)

In 1976, a Master Development Plan draft was completed. The Park was to be regional in scope and was to preserve the wilderness character and visual integrity of the land. A community-wide contest in 1979 resulted in the Park's name—Mission Trails Regional Park.

Fundraising, land acquisition and efforts to increase Park awareness were undertaken in the 1980s. By then, about 3,000 acres were already under various public ownerships—about half of today's total park acreage. Under the leadership of Nancy Acevedo of the Park and Recreation Department, an additional 2,500 acres were acquired from the Federal Government and private parties from 1981 through the 1990s, partially funded by open space bonds approved by voters as Proposition C in 1978. A final Master Development Plan was approved in 1985 by the San Diego City Council and San Diego County Board of Supervisors.

The Master Plan called for a visitor center; efforts in the early 1990s focused on raising funds toward that goal. In February 1995, the Park's spectacular Visitor and Interpretive Center opened, showcasing the magnificent terrain around it. The $5.5 million complex was paid for with corporate and private donations and state and local grants solicited by the Mission Trails Regional Park Foundation.

Historical and Cultural Features

Not only is MTRP valued for its open space and diversity of plants and animals in close proximity to an urban center, but the Park also contains several historical and cultural features as well:

- The Old Mission Dam, built over a 10 year period, is the first European water works in the Western United States, dedicated as a National Historical Landmark in 1971. It is easily accessible from both entrances of the Father Junipero Serra Trail, although some walking is required.

- Over 30 known Kumeyaay historical sites are located and protected within MTRP. Grinding sites, where those Indians who inhabited the park for generations processed their food, can be viewed up close in several locations on marked trails throughout the Park.

  A good concentration of these is located on an easily accessible trail that is a side trip off the Visitor Center Loop Trail or Father Junipero Serra Trail. There is another great place to see grinding rocks near the Grasslands Crossing junction along a trail heading towards Oak Canyon from the Grasslands Crossing.

- An important historical site, which is not generally available to visit is the Kumeyaay Winter Solstice Observatory on Cowles Mountain. However, Park docents lead hikes to this sacred Indian site in December each year around the time of the Winter Solstice, when the site aligns with the sunrise between two mountain peaks on the eastern horizon. A scale model of the observatory can also be viewed at the amphitheatre adjacent to the Visitor Center.

- No trip to the Park is complete without a stop at the Visitor and Interpretive Center located at One Father Junipero Serra Trail, just off Mission Gorge Road between Jackson Drive and Golfcrest Drive. As you approach the building, notice how well it suits the topography and natural colors of the landscape surrounding it. Winner of the ASLA's (American Society of Landscape Architects) Centennial Medallion as a National Landmark for Outstanding Landscape Architecture, the innovative design also garnered the City of San Diego's 1995 William Earl Hayden Award for Building Project of the Year. Project architect was Joseph Wong Design Associates. Landscape Architect was Kawasaki Theilacker Ueno and Associates. Soltek of San Diego was the General Contractor for the project.

This beautiful $5.5 million facility, which opened in 1995, was a joint project of the Mission Trails Regional Park Foundation, Inc., and the City of San Diego. Inside are permanent displays on the history of the Old Mission Dam and Kumeyaay people, as well as child-friendly interactive exhibits about MTRP plants and animals. Also, there is a resource library, an auditorium featuring video and multi-media presentations on the Park, beautiful artwork and photographs taken within Park boundaries. Staffed by friendly volunteers, Park Rangers, other City staff and Foundation employees, there is always someone willing to suggest a hike or answer a question.

᷍

BURROWING OWLS

CHAPTER 3

Come Face to Face with Nature in Many Different Forms

Many San Diegans are surprised to learn that there are more plant and animal species living in the San Diego/Baja California Region than in any other area of similar size in North America. In fact, other than Hawaii, there are more rare and endangered plant species in San Diego County than any other place in the nation.

The climate plays a role but so does the geology and geography of the area. For over two hundred million years, organisms have been adapting and evolving in the zone where the Pacific and North American tectonic plates meet. Over this same period, the climate has changed from tropical to subtropical to arid. Active volcanoes have been replaced by a rich and scenic coastline, eroded mountains and an exotic desert landscape. Each shift left behind plants and animals that have been able to adapt and even thrive under the new conditions.

In San Diego County, there are 16 different habitats (habitat=place where an organism lives) and 13 different micro-climate areas, creating the opportunities for all this biodiversity. Mission Trails Regional Park, as one of the largest open space urban parks in America, provides a wonderful opportunity to experience this diversity up close.

Native plant communities in MTRP

Excellent examples of five different terrestrial (land) habitats lie within the Park. The largest is **chaparral** and its subset, the **coastal sage scrub** community, which can be experienced in many places throughout the Park. According to Park staff, only two percent of the world's

biomes (a community of plants and animals that exist together) are chaparral, characterized by shrub plants that can withstand drought and fire. These grow only in Mediterranean-type climates like ours where there are cool, moist winters and hot, dry

MATILIJA POPPIES

summers with an average rainfall of 10 inches per year. During the summer and fall, some of these plants appear to be dead but are in fact, dormant. After just one day's gentle rain, shades of green can appear on hillsides that were here-to-fore brownish gray.

An interesting characteristic to look for in a chaparral/coastal sage community are adjacent hillsides with differing amounts of green foliage. This will vary depending on whether they are north or west-facing or south or east-facing. North or west-facing receive more moisture from coastal breezes and less intense sunlight, thereby producing a denser chaparral foliage than the warmer, drier conditions where the sparser coastal sage scrub vegetation grows. Coastal sage landscape predominates in Mission Trails Regional Park, as it used to throughout Southern California. Today it is estimated that from 70-90% of coastal sage habitat is gone due to high density housing developments in our region.

Common Chaparral/Coastal Sage Plants:

Some of the most common plants in the chapparal/coastal sage community include: **California sagebrush** with fragrant leaves similar to dill weed; **black sage** with larger leaves of a darker green color and pale lavender flower clusters that age into dark spheres; **white sage** with a downy, almost white foliage and white to pale lavender blooms; **laurel sumac**, an evergreen shrub with glossy, taco-shaped leaves and clusters of tiny white flowers in late spring; **lemonade berry**, a member of the sumac family that produces a sticky fruit with a sour taste from which a soothing drink can be made; **mission manzanita**, densely branched shrub with gray shredding bark, revealing reddish trunks of very hard wood; **coastal goldenbush**, a member of the sunflower family which blooms late spring to late fall. In autumn, its yellow flowers dominate the hill-sides and trail sides of the Park; **flat-top buckwheat**, featuring tiny white flowers with pink anthers most of the year, making it, along with the white and black sage, a valuable honey plant and popular insect nectar source nearly year-round; and the ubiquitous **broom baccharis**, an evergreen bush that blooms almost year-round with tiny white flowers which develop into a cottony fluff.

Chaparral or coastal sage scrub habitat is also a good place to look for two common types of yucca plants in MTRP: "**Our Lord's Candle**" with its single tall stalk of large white flowers and the **Mohave yucca** or **Spanish dagger/bayonet** with narrow, spiky leaves surrounding short stalks of white flowers. Both bloom in late spring and need the yucca moth for pollination.

Oak Woodlands

Oak woodland habitat, found along many of the trails in the Park, provides welcome shade for people as well as important shelter and food for many different types of animals. The most common oak trees found within the Park and coastal San Diego are the **coast live oaks**. These trees have deep roots which reach water far beneath the soil surface, even when surface water is not available. Therefore they often appear as dark green mounds on hillsides above water sources rather than the brighter green trees which grow right down at water's edge.

Engelmann oaks—the rarest oak in California—also grow in one known location within MTRP—along the Oak

Grove trail near the Visitor Center. These oaks are characterized by longer, lighter leaves than the coast live oaks and have longer, more slender acorns.

Scrub oaks, a smaller member of the evergreen oak family found in California, thrive on drier hillsides and are often confused with young coast live oaks or other evergreen plants that co-exist with them. A similar plant in Spain, nicknamed "chapparo" (or "shorty" in English) gave rise to the term "chaparral."

Other plants found in oak woodland habitat include several berry-bearing shrubs, all evergreens, such as the **hollyleaf cherry**, the **toyon** or **holly berry**, the **spiny redberry** or **buckthorn plant**, and the **blue elderberry tree**.

Birds and insects of many varieties thrive in this environment as well as small mammals heard scurrying about the undergrowth, but one must sit quietly to observe them as most are well-camouflaged and quite shy.

Riparian

The lush, riparian landscape seen along the San Diego River's edge in Mission Trails Regional Park today is very different than it was 100 years ago, prior to the building of the El Capitan dam

MULE DEER

upstream. Today, due to a steady stream of water year-round, it is a dense, wooded habitat made up of willows, sycamore and cottonwood trees.

This is one instance in which a man-made change yielded an environment well-suited for wildlife. Riparian woodlands provide vital habitat for a variety of animals including the **least Bell's vireo**, an endangered songbird. Other wildlife found here includes mammals such as **mule deer** and **raccoon**, along with songbirds like the **common yellowthroat**, **yellow-rumped warbler** and **Bullock's oriole**. California has lost over 90% of its riparian woodlands to development in the past century. This type of habitat is considered the most sensitive plant community in the country.

The **arroyo willow** loses its leaves in winter but other times of the year makes up a dense thicket near the river's edge and around Kumeyaay Lake. Historically, local Indians used its bark strips for skirts, flexible branches for building material and storage baskets, and brewed a pain-reliever similar to aspirin by soaking its bark in hot water. Although it is usually a shrub, these willows can grow into trees 30-feet tall. The **sandbar willow** and the **pacific willow** are two other members of the willow family that thrive near water sources within the Park.

Another common riparian plant is the **mule fat** shrub (also called **seep willow**), which has a leaf structure similar to that of the arroyo willow. However it is an evergreen plant with clusters of small white flower heads in spring and summer, rather than the catkins found on the willows. Mule fat is actually a member of the sunflower family.

Western sycamores, which can grow up to 90 ft. tall, also lose their leaves in fall and winter, revealing interesting structural shapes with white branches towards the top and mottled bark on the trunks lower down. Fruits are one-inch bristly spheres easily seen when branches are bare.

Cottonwood trees can be identified by their heart-shaped leaves, seen twisting and fluttering in a breeze around grey, deeply-furrowed trunks. **Black cottonwoods** (look for these right around the Visitor Center) feature leaves that are silvery green underneath and darker green on top, while the **Fremont cottonwoods**' leaves are more uniformly yellow green with round-toothed edges. As members of the willow family, both varieties produce catkins in the spring, which later yield capsules with cottony seeds that scatter in the fall. Leaves of the cottonwoods seen in Mission Trails turn a bright yellow in the fall in contrast to the dull browns and yellows of the sycamores around them.

Many of these same trees also grow in and around Kumeyaay Lake and Lake Murray. But while familiar riparian trees and shrubs can be found along with tall stands of **broad-leaved cattails** (an emergent aquatic plant) around these reliable sources of water, these are sometimes choked out by **giant reeds** that also populate the marshy edges of the static manmade lakes.

Giant reeds or arundo, members of the grass family resembling bamboo, can grow to 15 ft. tall. This invasive plant was introduced from Europe and has managed to spread to riparian and aquatic habitats throughout most of California. While unwelcome as a non-native, the dense vegetation it helps create does attract insects, algae and other smaller forms of life (invertebrates) – welcome food sources for the aquatic wildlife that proliferates in an aquatic environment.

Park staff, with the help of contractors and volunteers, have nearly eradicated the giant reed from the Park. In fact, according to Ranger Paul Seiley in 2001, "The stretch of the San Diego River running through Mission Trails is probably the most pristine to be found between the ocean and the Cleveland National Forest."

Grasslands

There are two areas within MTRP where you can explore a grasslands habitat: East Fortuna on the Santee side and West Fortuna on the Tierrasanta side. Unlike the riparian and oak woodlands habitats, these are wide-open spaces where views are unimpeded and wildlife can be easily viewed if one is patient. Commonly found plants include native grasses such as **purple needle grass**, **California buckwheat**, **Indian ricegrass** and **basket grass**, but also grasses introduced by Europeans for grazing animals such as **wild oats**, **red** and **white clovers**, **foxtails** and the **filarees**. Most California perennial native grasses have been replaced by Old World annual species.

Insects, such as crickets and grasshoppers and those animals that prey on them thrive in the grasslands of MTRP. The openness of the terrain makes this a great venue for spotting native and migrating birds, lizards, rabbits, ground squirrels and other rodents and even mule deer.

Grass plants have extensive roots that go deep underground, protecting them from complete eradication by grazing animals. In fact, more than two-thirds of the plant can be found underground! Because they grow from the base of the plant rather than the tips and can regenerate after extensive drought conditions and even wildfires by using nutrients stored in their root system, grasses survive well under harsh conditions.

Throughout the Park

WILDFLOWERS — In spring, especially after a rainy winter season, wildflowers carpet the grasslands habitat (and many other areas of the Park)–most commonly the **California poppy**, **baby blue eyes**, **black mustard*** and **red bush monkeyflower**. But you might also discover **St. John's wort, common star lilies, leafy stem coreopsis, Queen Anne's lace, sweet fennel*** and **California goldfields**. It's

CALIFORNIA POPPIES

also possible during spring months to catch a glimpse of the largest flower of any native California plant: the spectacular white and yellow **Coulter's matilija poppy**.

If you're especially interested in wildflowers, stop by the Gift Shop area in the Visitor and Interpretive Center to buy a colorful brochure entitled "Flowering Plants of Mission Trails Regional Park." Over 60 varieties are identified with clear, good-size photos and the dates when they bloom in the Park. *Hint: There is always something blooming, although the peak wildflower season is obviously in the early spring if San Diego has had decent rainfall during the winter months!*

CACTI — Although they also dwell among chaparral/coastal sage scrub plants, the open grasslands of MTRP are your best bet to spot **barrel cactus** as well as **beavertail** and **short coastal prickly pear cacti**, and the **teddybear** or **jumping cholla**, with its short, fuzzy-looking branches.

PARASITIC PLANTS — Less prevalent, but also residing in MTRP are several varieties of parasitic plants such as mistletoe and California dodder.

FERNS AND FUNGI — In the shadier, moister areas, it's also possible to spot ferns, moss, algae, lichen and many varieties of fungi including mushrooms.

From Crawling Insects to Soaring Hawks, Animals Abound in MTRP

On a recent hike near Kumeyaay Lake the author and a friend were startled by the appearance of two healthy adult mule deer moving silently across our path and into the dense vegetation at the lake's edge. We were still congratulating ourselves for choosing this hike on this gorgeous autumn day, when three more deer suddenly appeared: a stag, a doe and a fawn. They too disappeared quickly and silently. Five deer in the span of a few minutes! The author has lived in Southern California for twenty-seven years, her friend is a native San Diegan, but neither had ever been this close to a large animal species in the wild. It was hard to believe that a 15-minute drive from MTRP, other friends were celebrating Octoberfest in the Gaslamp Quarter of downtown San Diego!

Although mule deer are a protected species, they are fairly easy to see in the San Diego County backcountry more than an hour's drive away from the urban center, but it is also possible to come face to face with one on any given day in Mission Trails Regional Park…

Important Lessons from Nature

Bats, myotis (members of the bat family), **kangaroo rats, skunks, weasels, shrews, coyotes, bobcats**–even **cougars**–all make their home in MTRP. Of course these animals range from the middle to the top of the food chain. But there are also thousands of different insect species, including a rare **termite** species that was discovered within the Park's boundaries recently.

Songbirds nest in grasslands and rodents burrow underground to feed on roots and seeds. Coyotes and hawks can be seen as they search the area for prey. Another good site for spotting birds are the sheer, exposed cliffs of abandoned sand and gravel quarry sites within Mission Trails. There you might see the **great-horned owls, red-tailed hawks, common ravens, white-throated swifts** and **canyon wrens** that nest and roost there. The cool wood-lands provide respite for migrating birds like the colorful **western tanager** and **Townsend's warbler** as they feed and rest before continuing their long journey to the tropical forests of Mexico, Central and South America in the fall or back to northern climes in the spring.

If you're hiking in an oak woodland habitat area you might also spot the **arboreal salamander** or acorn-collecting **scrub jays** in the daytime, hear the **spotted towhees** rustling about in the underbrush or the **Pacific tree frogs** as dusk begins to fall. Watch for spiders spinning webs backlit by morning sun or rabbits and ground squirrels scurrying across the trail in front of you.

Park Ranger Luanne Barrett never tires of the diversity surrounding her in MTRP. "Most of us have certain smells that trigger a response in us–like trees after rain, campfires–these things strike a chord in our nature that is important. There is something primitive about it. It's why we're drawn to water and nature."

Everyone on the MTRP staff agrees that one of the most important things they do is pass on their knowledge to the younger generation.

"The only smells kids today know is hot asphalt and bus fumes. How is that going to bring back pleasant memories?" Luanne asks.

"There are plenty of opportunities if you just make the effort to instill in kids the responsibilities to the earth and fellow man, and show them what miracles are around us every day."

She shares this knowledge in classes about tracking animals and nature hikes with campers at Kumeyaay Lake Campground. "The more people know, the better; to care about something, they have to understand it." She urges visitors to take advantage of all the free programs available in the Park: trail guide walks, native plant walks, bird watching expeditions, star parties, Indian programs, etc.

Ranger Rick Thompson, who was involved for several years in a state project for community service, feels kids programs are undoubtedly the most valuable.

COMMON RAVEN

"If we can win the kids, we will ensure that stewardship will happen for decades to come. If we can generate the same kind of love and enthusiasm as we have – that's a job well done."

Look and Listen

During the hot, dry summer months animals that live in the coastal sage scrub habitat such as the deer mouse, coyote and red diamond rattlesnake will sleep in burrows or in the shade during the hottest part of the day, coming out in the cooler morning and evening hours. These are also the best times to look for the many varieties of bats and for barn owls living in the Park.

Even the staff gets excited when they spot rare species. Park Ranger Mel Naidas was enthusing over a very rare green heron he encountered recently and in the past two years has reported several sightings of a pair of golden eagles in and around the Park.

Around Kuymeyaay Lake or the narrow stream along the Oak Grove Trail near the Visitor Center watch for butterflies and dragonflies that hover near the water. Dense willow thickets along the water's edge also provide nesting, safety and food for many local animals such as the endangered least Bell's vireo.

Less easy to find, but an incredible spectacle for those lucky enough to see one are the vernal pools sometimes found on the top of bedrock plateaus. Grounds Maintenance Worker Tom Folk considers it one of the fringe benefits of working out in the Park to have seen them.

"You wouldn't believe how much life is in there! It's like a miniature lake with a miniature city inside."

But he strongly cautioned against disturbing this very fragile habitat. "The fairy shrimp, plants and spade foot tadpoles found in these tiny pockets of water are interdependent."

Park Ranger Casey Smith agrees, reporting that only one out of 800 tadpoles makes it to adulthood. "Sometimes the little frogs, which develop toes and lungs within a one-hour time frame and have to quickly make it to dry land, drown in an indentation made by a human foot."

"While this may not seem that significant, in fact, the successful periodic regeneration of vernal pools is essential for other wildlife in the area such as foxes and deer."

Descending from Cowles Mountain on a late spring afternoon, listen for the coyotes and their kits hidden in the brush but preparing for a night of hunting on the eastern slopes. Near the Grasslands Crossing, search for the elusive **western meadowlark**, whose lyrical song is easily heard while the colorful bird itself is difficult to see.

*For photo credits,
see page 135.*

Variety of Animals That Frequent MTRP

Following is a condensed list of some of the species of animal life you might encounter on a hike in MTRP. Taking along a small pair of binoculars, a magnifying glass and a field guide with photos will make identification easier. Several good ones are available for sale at the Visitor Center.

Insects...dragonflies, scarab beetles, true bugs, ants, bees, walking sticks, tarantulas, scorpions, termites, butterflies and moths.

Other invertebrates...worms, crayfish, snails and slugs.

Fish...bluegill, large-mouth bass, California catfish, crappie, rainbow trout (stocked in Lake Murray)*, red-ear sunfish, and yellow bullhead.

Amphibians...banded geckos, tree frogs, bullfrogs, toads.

Reptiles...horned lizards, whiptails, skinks, alligator lizards, snakes and turtles.

Birds...raptors including ospreys, red-tailed and red-shouldered hawks, Cooper's hawks, golden eagles and peregrine falcons; crows and ravens; owls; woodpeckers; songbirds, including two endangered species: the California gnatcatcher and the least Bell's vireo; several varieties of hummingbirds; native shorebirds; egrets and herons; as well as many species of migrating birds.

Are you a dedicated birder or just a novice? For a small donation, pick up a brochure that lists over 200 species of birds that have been recorded in MTRP. It lists where

CALIFORNIA
GNATCATCHER

each was spotted and whether it lives and nests in the Park like the ring-tailed pheasant, or just passes through during migration like the common loon. Use the checklist and record your own sightings—especially any rare or new species you find—and return it to the Visitor Center.

Mammals…gophers, squirrels, chipmunks, grasshopper mice, rabbits, hares, kangaroo rats, wood rats, California voles, bats, skunks, raccoons, deer, foxes, weasels, coyotes, bobcats, shrews, and even cougars (mountain lions).

Marsupial…opposum*

Protected Species

The follwing plants and animals are protected under the Multiple Species Conservation Plan Rules and Guidelines (1997).

<u>**Plants**</u>	<u>**Animals**</u>
Encinitas baccharis	burrowing owl
Orcutt's brodiaea	California gnatcatcher
Palmer's ericameria	California rufous-crowned sparrow
San Diego ambrosia	Cooper's hawk
San Diego barrel cactus	least Bell's vireo
San Diego goldenstar	Southern mule deer
San Diego thornmint	orange-throated whiptail

slender-pod jewelflower	San Diego horned lizard
variegated dudleya	tricolored blackbird
willowy monardella	Western bluebird

asterisk indicates non-native plants or animals

Maintaining an Urban "Open Space" Park

By its very name, "open space" implies that one can go wherever one wishes in such a park, but in fact the opposite is true. Because the space is shared with many wild creatures and threatened plant-life there must be rules and regulations governing the Park's usage. The difficulty comes in trying to maintain a healthy balance between regulating people's behaviors to protect the environment while also providing access to the wonders of nature. Hopefully this access will encourage people to develop a greater appreciation of, and respect for, the environment and cultural resources which need protection.

The staff and volunteers of Mission Trails Regional Park always seek to strike this balance and, for that reason, constantly monitor trails, habitat areas, and historic sites to make sure that visitors and their pets are staying on the trails and out of the sensitive areas. This is especially important since several endangered plant and animal species exist within the Park's boundaries. For example, the least Bell's vireo builds its nests low to the ground in willow thickets in several locations within the Park. During nesting season, access to certain trails may be restricted.

When an area is deemed no longer sensitive and can be re-opened to visitors, the barriers will most likely be removed. (However, in certain areas, like Kumeyaay Lake, the sensitive area remains closed year-round to protect the habitat for the following year's nesting season.)

Many housing developments border MTRP, presenting another challenge for Park staff and volunteers. Non-native plants, such as grasses introduced long ago by early European settlers and tropical exotics "transplanted" by nature with wind-borne seeds from backyard gardens bordering the Park's boundaries, compete with local plant species for water and space. In turn, animals that depend on the native plants as food sources also become threatened. In the last dozen years there has been a concerted effort to replace these plant species with native varieties in many areas of the Park.

Living on a wild canyon or hillside bordering the Park gives homeowners more privacy and sometimes breathtaking vistas, even increasing property value. But this privilege also carries with it a responsibility. Not planting exotic plants near the canyon's edge, nor allowing dogs and cats to wander unleashed into the Park are fairly simple rules for good neighborliness. Knowledge of Park management issues, as well as native plant and animal species, will help preserve the treasure that is MTRP for future generations.

How to Protect Plant and Animal Life

- Follow signs and <u>stay on the marked trails at all times</u>
- Stay out of sensitive habitat areas
- <u>Dogs must be on leash at all times</u>
- Clean up after your dog (baggies for this purpose may be available at some trailheads)
- Do not feed any wild animals you encounter
- Do not allow your pets to wander off into the brush or canyons surrounding residential areas
- <u>If you live in a home bordering the parklands,</u> try planting native plants in your backyard and never use fertilizers, fungicides, or insecticides that will be harmful to animals. Do not leave pet food outside overnight. Close trash containers securely
- Don't ever take any plant or animal specimens from the Park
- Do not release any domesticated animals in the Park
- Take out what you bring with you, or dispose of properly
- "Take only photographs; leave only footprints…"

CHAPTER 4

Before You Go (Practicalities)
Places to Stay, Buy Supplies and Eat Breakfast

Ideally, whether you are a resident of San Diego County or an out-of-state visitor, you should consider camping within MTRP at Kumeyaay Lake Campground off Mission Gorge Road near Santee. Not only are you able to roast marshmallows and enjoy scheduled weekend campfire talks by Park Rangers, Park docents and wildlife experts, but you will sleep under a carpet of stars and wake

*RED BUSH
MONKEYFLOWER*

to the sounds of hundreds of birds, including the many native and migrating species that populate the grasslands and riparian habitat surrounding the campground. In the morning, take a hike, explore the Old Mission Dam or go on a mountain biking excursion to a very different type of habitat. All within eight miles of downtown San Diego!

Recreational vehicles are permitted overnight in the campground but there are no hook-ups in the Park. During nesting season, between March 15 and September 15, generators are not allowed anywhere in the Park but may be used at other times of the year. However, generators are never allowed at campsites adjacent to the Lake. The campground is best suited for tent camping. Two tents per camp site are permitted. Grills, picnic tables, bathroom and shower facilities with hot and cold water are all available. There is one covered pavilion lakeside for large group picnicking (check with Park staff for availability and any fees). Day use of the campground is permitted as long as space is available.

Nearby Hotels

If camping is just not your style, the two best places to find hotel accommodations close to MTRP are Mission Valley in San Diego and along Fletcher Parkway in La Mesa. These two areas are each less than five miles away from the Visitor and Interpretive Center on Father Junipero Serra Trail and offer several different choices for inexpensive but comfortable family lodging. If you wish to find something a bit more upscale, then Mission Valley is your best bet with a Marriott, Hilton and Red Lion in close proximity. There are also several resort-style properties at the west end of the valley with swimming pools and golf courses.

Food Options

Since the best times to view wildlife in the Park are early morning and early evening, grab a cup of coffee and a muffin from the continental breakfast bar at your hotel and head to the Park for a brisk hike or bike ride before the Visitor and Interpretive Center opens at 9 a.m. Then stop in for a current map and guide to that day's programs, before heading out to a hearty breakfast at the Omelette Factory in Santee, Coco's Restaurant in Grantville or Earth

Blend Coffee and Tea on Santo Road in Tierrasanta. Pick up bottled water, deli sandwiches, fruit and cookies or trail mix before returning to the Park for further exploration and a picnic lunch.

The closest Subway sandwich shop is located at the intersection of West Hills Parkway and Mission Gorge Road near the north end of Father Junipero Serra Trail. Two other good places to stock up on supplies are the Mission Trails Market at the intersection of Jackson Drive and Mission Gorge Rd., close to the Visitor and Interpretive Center, and the Farmers' Outlet Market on Santo Rd., near the main West Fortuna entrance in Tierrasanta.

Planning a serious hike to the top of Cowles Mountain or Pyles Peak? Take plenty of bottled water and a nutrition bar, available from Cheers Deli or Keil's Market at the corner of Navajo Road and Jackson Drive. A great place for breakfast or lunch afterwards is Megan's Cafe in the same shopping center.

If you're planning a visit to Lake Murray, you'll find two very good breakfast and lunch places near the Kiowa Dr. entrance—Coco's Restaurant on Lake Murray Blvd., or the Baltimore Cafe at the intersection of Lake Murray Blvd. and Baltimore Drive. There's also a Subway sandwich shop and a quick market/deli located on the east side of Lake Murray Blvd., between the exit off Interstate 8 for Lake Murray Blvd. and Kiowa Dr. Across I-8, on the south side of the freeway, is a Denny's Restaurant and a Marie Callender's restaurant (open for breakfast only on weekends). All offer take-out options for picnics. Just remember that this is a city park. No glass containers or consumption of alcoholic beverages are permitted, and you must remove or dispose of all trash properly.

Planning Your Visit

Check Internet, www.mtrp.org

Before any trip to MTRP, spend time studying the excellent Web site available on the Internet: *www.mtrp.org*. The Web site's user-friendly format will guide you to discover more about the specific area you want to visit or the activity you're most interested in. The staff and volunteers offer a continually changing array of programs for every age group. The best way to find out about current offerings is to check their calendar of events for the week you're planning to visit.

Bird-watching, stargazing parties, plant identification, geology and Spanish history walks, animal tracking classes and Native American musical concerts are just a few of the opportunities that might be available at the time of your visit. Most of these are led by expert Trail Guides, educators or Park Rangers. Some are offered specifically for young children and disabled visitors. A private walking tour for a group of 10 or more people with a volunteer Trail Guide (docent) may be arranged at least two weeks in advance by calling Ranger staff at (619) 668-3279. You may also be able to obtain specific information for your visit through personal e-mail contact with the staff. Field trip information for school groups is also available at www.mtrp.org/fieldtrips or by calling the Education Ranger staff at (619) 668-3279.

Determining how much time you need for a visit will depend on the size of your group and the type of activity you wish to engage in. Allow at least one hour for a complete visit to the Visitor and Interpretive Center, including time to enjoy a video and slide presentations about the Park and a self-guided stroll along a native plant identification walk.

Regularly scheduled Trail Guide walks, with a trained volunteer naturalist, start at the Visitor Center every Wednesday, Saturday and Sunday at 9:30 a.m., and last about one and a half hours. If you're in great shape, you can also hike to the top of Cowles Mountain and back in that amount of time. But it's also possible to spend an entire morning or afternoon in the Park on a long meandering walk that takes you from one wildlife community to another, enjoying a picnic along the way.

MATILIJA POPPY

If you're a rock climber or mountain biker, your time in the Park depends on the time and energy you have to devote to your sport. You could spend a few hours or an entire day. Ideally, no trip should be rushed. Literally, "take time to smell the flowers" and to realize what a very special place this is. In fact, breathe deeply. And because it's so close to the urban center, visit often.

What to Wear

Dress comfortably according to the current weather conditions and time of year. Layers are almost always best. Summer and fall are the hottest and driest months, but even then it's possible to get chilled after doing a steep climb in the sun when you find yourself coming down the east side of a mountain toward the end of the day. San Diego can also turn cool and breezy with a sudden shift in the wind from the desert to the ocean, bringing in a marine layer of clouds that blocks the sun. Pack a light long-sleeved shirt or sweater to slip on over your sleeveless tee-shirt and you'll be fine. Light weight pants or shorts will be most comfortable in summer and fall while jeans or other long pants are suitable for the winter or spring months. Sturdy shoes and socks are a must year-round.

Health and Safety Matters

For moderate to easy trails, running or walking shoes are fine; for steeper trails, hiking boots or walking shoes with more tread are recommended. During the dry season, many of the trails have areas of decomposed granite that require extra caution, particularly during a quick descent. Alternately, mud and shallow streams may need to be forded in winter and early spring after seasonal rains.

Helmets should always be worn by mountain bicyclists and appropriate attire used by equestrians and rock climbers. Everyone should wear sunscreen year-round in our climate as well as a fanny-pack or lightweight backpack to **carry plenty of water.** A broad-brimmed hat or cap is recommended for hikers and horsebackriders. If possible, always carry a small pair of binoculars—you'll definitely regret it if you're on a trail, see an unusual bird or rock formation and you've neglected to pack them.

For safety on a long hike, particularly if you're alone, take a cell phone. In addition, anyone planning a long hike alone on remote trails should be aware of safety; consider carrying a whistle. Although the risks are few and the rewards great, hiking with a companion is always the safest way to enjoy MTRP.

Bringing Your Dog to MTRP

Finally, if you're bringing your dog to Mission Trails Regional Park, it must be on a leash! As a former veterinarian's assistant, Ranger Sue Pelley recalls some of the painful effects of cactus and foxtails on dogs wandering unleashed and off-trail. In addition, besides the ever present danger of rattlesnake bite (two dogs a year are lost in San Diego due to snake bites), ticks and the common discomfort of poison oak, which is easily transferred to the dog's owner, there is also the potential for damage to sensitive habitat and encounters with other, not-so-friendly, dogs.

"Even though your dog may be very well-trained and will heel for the entire walk, you are sending the wrong message to other dog owners whose dogs may not be so well-trained. Sadly, a few hair-raising incidents have spoiled many a dog walker's (not to mention his dog's) day," reminds Ranger Pelley. If this isn't enough to deter you, keep in mind that you could also be ticketed with a fine of up to $250 for having your dog off-leash anywhere in Mission Trails Regional Park.

Park Etiquette

Why Rules and Restrictions

In interviewing the staff and volunteers at MTRP, it is obvious they are sincerely dedicated to preserving and protecting this park's natural, historic and cultural resources for future generations of San Diegans, and for the plants and animals that inhabit it. Occasionally they have to deal with people who have been used to traipsing all over the land wherever they wish and doing whatever they like.

In most cases when a Park visitor is given more information about the delicate balance of the ecosystem and the reason for the rules and regulations, they are more than happy to comply. Often, these frequent Park users become its most ardent defenders and volunteers. Unfortunately, a minority contingent need to be reminded of the rules and regulations and, sometimes, even fined for offenses.

Park Ranger Rick Thompson made the most compelling case for protection of this rare resource. "If the circle of life were a pyramid, the top and bottom must be present for the pyramid to be healthy. Mission Trails Regional Park represents a healthy pyramid today. Both the top predators (mountain lions, coyotes and bobcats), and the large herbivores (such as mule deer) they prey upon, are healthy and abundant in this Park today.

"That means all the other links in the food chain are also existent and healthy. If one link begins to weaken, the pyramid crumbles and falls. In order to maintain a healthy Park, the animals must have places where they feel safe and secure and they must have an on-going dependable food source."

Remembering the shortage of coastal sage scrub habitat still left in California, and the number of endangered plants and animals that co-exist in this type of habitat, it is especially important to follow some basic rules of not just etiquette, but stewardship, while visiting Mission Trails Regional Park.

Do's

- Do bring picnic foods to enjoy while exploring MTRP. But remember to carry out all trash and scraps. Trash cans and recycling containers are available near most trailheads.
- Do take lots of photographs but leave the wildflowers to reseed and for others to enjoy. Do not remove any plants, animals or Indian artifacts you find in Mission Trails.
- Obey signs concerning unexploded ordnance. The Park's prior usage as a military practice target range is well documented. Sweeps have been made to detect and remove any leftover unexploded shells. However, you could still come across one–

particularly after a heavy rain. DO NOT TOUCH!!
Call 911 and stay nearby until help arrives.

- Always stay on marked trails. Obey signs marking
  sensitive habitat areas and stay out of these, even
  if there are apparent signs of an old trail leading
  through an area. Re-vegetation is occurring in
  many areas of the Park.

- Always watch for hikers or climbers emerging from
  side paths onto your trail.

- Bring your dog(s) to MTRP, but always and
  everywhere in the Park keep them on a leash. You
  never know when you may encounter another dog
  that is not as friendly or well-behaved as yours.

- Pick up after your pet. Baggies for this purpose may
  be available within the Park (best to bring your own),
  and trash cans are located near most trailheads.

- On any trail, walkers and joggers should move to
  the right and walk or run single file when signaled
  by a mountain biker or horseback rider that they
  wish to pass.

- If mountain biking, the official speed limit is
  10 miles per hour. It is especially important to
  observe speed limits on blind curves where hikers
  or horseback riders share the trail.

- Be aware of posted hours for gated areas and be
  sure to move your parked car before the gates are
  closed and locked for the night.

- Mountain bikers should yield to horses by pulling
  over to the side and stopping to let the horse and
  rider pass. For this and other rules of the trail, refer

to the San Diego Mountain Bike Association's Web site: www.sdmba.com.

Don'ts

- Never take short cuts through the brush in the flat areas or to shorten a climb on steep switchback trails. "Where one goes, others will follow."
- Drive your car no more than 15 miles per hour on Father Junipero Serra Trail and only in the northerly direction permitted through Mission Gorge.
- The left side of Father Junipero Serra Trail (heading north) is reserved for walkers, joggers, and bicyclists only. Cars are permitted only on the right and only going in a northerly direction from the Visitor Center area toward the Old Mission Dam and Kumeyaay Lake Campground.
- Open fires are not allowed anywhere in the Park, unless under Park staff supervision.
- Kite-flying or radio controlled vehicles are not allowed in MTRP. Ask the staff about other parks or areas nearby where such activities are permitted.
- Never let your child or pet wander off in the brush that borders the trails. Not only is this harmful to the Park's sensitive habitat, but is also dangerous for your companion. Rattlesnakes are a common sight in the Park and can defensively strike at your child or pet if disturbed.
- Do not feed the animals, including birds that might be attracted to your picnic. Human food is not

good for them and may, over time, discourage them from foraging for regular foods in their diet.

- Refrain from activity that is clearly not allowed in certain areas and on certain trails, i.e., not mountain biking or horseback riding on trails reserved for hiking only.

- Don't bring firearms; they are not permitted within MTRP.

Driving Directions

The Park is accessible from several different locations. The next chapter includes a description of each region of the Park and the type of activity that can be best enjoyed in each region. There is also a fold-out map showing major freeway and street access to each area in the back of this book.

Directions to the Mission Gorge region of MTRP, including the Visitor Center and Old Mission Dam:

From Interstate 8 or Interstate 15 — Take I-8 (East or West) to I-15 North. From I-15, exit on Friars Road East, which turns into Mission Gorge Road. Where the two roads intersect, follow Mission Gorge east for 4.2 miles. Look for the large wooden Mission Trails Regional Park sign on the left side of Mission Gorge Road, just past a stop light at Jackson Drive.

Turn left onto Father Junipero Serra Trail. To reach the Visitor and Interpretive Center, turn left before the pipe gate on Father Junipero Serra Trail and continue up the concrete driveway. The Center will be to your right. To the left, off the driveway, are two sections of off-street parking. (Note: Visitor Center access gates to these parking lots are locked at 5 p.m. daily, year-round.)

If you are going to Old Mission Dam, continue past the pipe gate (open 8 a.m.-5 p.m. daily from November through March; 8 a.m.-7 p.m., April through October) down Father Junipero Serra Trail. The entrance to the Dam is 1.8 miles down the road just past the second pipe gate.

Directions to the East Fortuna Region:

From State Route 125 or State Route 52 — Take SR125 to SR52 West. From SR52 (East or West) exit on Mast Blvd. in Santee. To enter the Grasslands area from Mast Blvd., go south (underneath the freeway if you were driving west on 52; simply turn right if you were heading east), park on either side of the street. Mast Blvd. dead-ends here at the Park entrance.

To begin your exploration on the Father Junipero Serra Trail, or to find the Kumeyaay Lake Campground after you exit Route 52, go north to the first traffic signal (West Hills Parkway) and turn right. Take West Hills Parkway to Mission Gorge Road and turn right. Proceed down Mission Gorge Road 0.2 miles and turn right onto Father Junipero Serra Trail. The entrance to the lake and campground is 0.2 miles down the road on the right and the entrance to the Grasslands Loop trail from this side is a bit further, also on the right, between the Campground entrance and the Old

Mission Dam. There is also a parking lot at the intersection of Bushy Hill Drive and Father Junipero Serra Trail.

From Interstate 15 or Interstate 8 — Take I-8 (East or West) to I-15 North. From I-15, exit on Friars Road East, which turns into Mission Gorge Road. Where the two roads intersect, follow Mission Gorge east for 4.2 miles, whre you will see the entrance to the Visitor Center and Father Junipero Serra Trail on the left. DO NOT TURN HERE, but proceed further on Mission Gorge Road 2.4 miles to the northeast entrance of Father Junipero Serra Trail. Turn left onto Father Junipero Serra Trail. The entrance to the Kumeyaay Lake Campground is 0.2 miles down the road on the right and the entrance to the Grasslands Loop trail is a bit further, but also on the right, between the Campground entrance and the Old Mission Dam. There is also a parking lot at the intersection of Bushy Hill Drive and Father Junipero Serra Trail.

To reach the Mast Blvd. entrance to the Park, DO NOT TURN ON Father Junipero Serra Trail; instead stay on Mission Gorge Road to the first stoplight past the turn for Father Junipero Serra Trail. Turn left on West Hills Parkway. Go to Mast Blvd. and turn left. You will pass underneath Route 52. Park on either side of the street. Mast Blvd. dead ends at this entrance to the Park. (A new parking area and picnic facilities will be constructed here in the near future.)

Directions to Cowles Mountain

Cowles Mtn. is located in the San Carlos area of San Diego, with primary access at the intersection of Navajo Rd. and Golfcrest Dr. But it is also possible to hike or bike the mountain from Barker Way. There are also two trailheads in Santee off Mission Gorge Road. (Refer to the map at the back of this book to find these trailheads.)

From the Visitor & Interpretive Center — Turn right onto Mission Gorge Road from Father Junipero Serra Trail and go to the first stoplight to make a U-turn in order to head east on Mission Gorge Road. Drive up the hill to the next stoplight and turn right on Golfcrest. CAUTION!! Speed limit is 25 mph on this residential street. Proceed slowly up the hill to a major intersection at Navajo Road and the hikers staging area, which will be on your left.

WESTERN FENCE LIZARD

From Interstate 8 —
Going east or west on I-8, exit on College Avenue and go north on College (away from SDSU). After passing through two stoplights you will come to a major intersection with Navajo Rd. Turn right on Navajo and continue to the intersection with Golfcrest Drive where you will see the staging area for hiking on this side of Cowles Mtn. Turn left and park along Golfcrest or turn off Golfcrest into a parking lot near restroom facilities.

From State Route 125 — Heading north or south on SR125, exit on Navajo Rd. and go west on Navajo through several stoplights to an intersection with Golfcrest Dr. Turn right and park on the street or into a parking lot off of Golfcrest.

Directions to the West Fortuna Region

From Interstate 15 or Interstate 8 — From I-8 (East or West) take I-15 North. From I-15, exit on Clairemont Mesa Blvd., going east. Follow Clairemont Mesa Blvd. all the way to the end where you'll find the main trailhead for this region. Park either outside the chain gate or inside, depending on how late you will be staying in the Park. Gate is locked at 7 p.m.

From State Route 125 or State Route 52 — From SR125 North, take SR52 West. From SR52 (East or West) take Santo Road exit in Tierrasanta. Proceed south on Santo Road to Clairemont Mesa Blvd. and turn left. Follow it to the end for parking and the trailhead.

Directions to Lake Murray (hiking/biking path and fishing)

From Interstate 8 (East or West) — Exit on Lake Murray Blvd. heading north to Kiowa Drive and turn left (drive-thru Starbucks on the corner!).

From the Visitor Center — Turn right from Father Junipero Serra Trail onto Mission Gorge Rd. Immediately get in left-hand lane and turn left on Jackson Drive. Go up the hill, cross Navajo Rd., and continue on Jackson, past Golfcrest, to Lakeshore Drive. Turn right on Lakeshore which becomes Baltimore. At Lake Murray Blvd. turn right and continue to Kiowa Dr. Turn right on Kiowa to entrance and parking for Lake Murray.

There is also access to the northeast end of Lake Murray from a residential neighborhood in San Carlos off Murray Park Dr. (See map inside the back cover.)

Start at Visitor and Interpretive Center

If you've never been there before, **make the Visitor and Interpretive Center your first stop**. Besides the great exhibits and films offered there, which will further introduce you to the Park's wonders; there are many walks, most moderate, and access to all the biking and even climbing trails in close proximity.

The Visitor and Interpretive Center is open every day from 9 a.m. to 5 p.m., except Thanksgiving, Christmas and New Year's Day. Follow the signs to the entrance, enjoying the interactive sound exhibits along the way. Once inside, the exhibit halls are to the left just past the information desk. But before you start, ask one of the volunteers when the next video or slide presentation will begin in the auditorium.

The importance of water in Mission Trails Regional Park is a major theme throughout the exhibit areas. Water carved the Gorge, attracted the Kumeyaay and the Spanish missionaries, and continues to support a variety of plant and animal life. On the first floor you'll find a diorama of the Old Mission Dam, a seismograph which registers earth tremors in our region, and Kumeyaay cultural exhibits. Don't miss the ramp leading to a glass viewing area overlooking the Gorge and, at the top, on the second floor, several audio-visual kiosks that will teach children more about wildlife found in the Park and the importance of protecting their habitat. For older children and adults, look for a display on the geology of the Park and the significance of the San Diego River as a watershed.

There is an outside viewing deck on this level and a broad terrace below, across from the main entrance. Both offer stunning views of the Park. Either exit on the main floor will take you to the Native Plant Identification Walk (ask a volunteer for a self-guided tour brochure), a beautiful flowing water feature representing the Old Flume, and an outdoor amphitheater.

Before you leave, be sure to visit the well-stocked reference library and wildlife-themed gift shop, and enjoy the artwork, photographs and sculpture displayed throughout the main corridor.

CHAPTER 5

What to See and Do

with contributions by Clark Rasmussen

Five Regions: Descriptions and Trail Info

The five regions are named for geographical features in each area. Three of the names are self-explanatory: **Mission Gorge, Cowles Mountain** and **Lake Murray**. But the names of the other two areas can be confusing for a first-time visitor. For clarification, the first two regions described in this chapter, **West Fortuna** and **East Fortuna**, get their names from two mountain *peaks*, "North Fortuna" and "South Fortuna," which are joined by a ridge called the "Fortuna Saddle." This ridge (or saddle) divides the western most part of the Park from the eastern area.

A simple map in the back of this book will show you the regions and major features of the Park along with the major access roads to reach them.

As you can see on the map, it is quite possible to cover a lot of territory and move from one region to the other, if you have several hours to spend. If you are hiking and don't wish to retrace your steps and want to experience as much of the Park as possible in one day, try taking a companion and two cars, dropping one off at the designated parking area at the end of Clairemont Mesa Boulevard in Tierrasanta, and the other on Mast Blvd. in Santee. Start your exploration in the Grasslands area of East Fortuna, visit the Old Mission Dam, then proceed up Oak Canyon to the service road that will take you up and over the Fortuna Mountain Saddle, down through Suycott Wash and up the other side to your car parked on Clairemont Mesa Blvd. Then return to Santee via Route 52 to pick up the second car.

An alternative plan would be to have someone drop you off at the parking lot and trailhead at Jackson Drive. Hike across the river and up the steep service road before dropping down a trail to Suycott Wash. Rest and enjoy a picnic in the tree-filled canyon at the southern part of the Wash before climbing a ridge and ascending the steps on the steep face of South Fortuna Mountain and dropping down to the Saddle and the East Fortuna region on the service road leading through the Grasslands to Mast Blvd. in Santee for pick-up at this entrance to the Park.

From an overlook near the top of South Fortuna, Ranger Mel Naidas' favorite spot, you can see the full extent of the Gorge and almost "go back in time."

"You don't see civilization if you look east, southeast of southwest. Instead you can see how the river went, how high it got and what life must have been like in the Gorge before the road went through..." If there are good winter rains, this is also one of the best areas in the spring to see wildflowers according to former Senior Ranger Paul Kilburg.

Or have someone drop you off at the Visitor Center, walk down Father Junipero Serra Trail (taking a side trip to the Grinding Rocks by the River) to the Old Mission Dam, up Oak Canyon to the service road leading up to the Fortuna Mountain Saddle and one of the mountain summits before proceeding down and across Suycott Wash and up the other side to either trailhead in West Fortuna where you can have someone pick you up at Clairemont Mesa or Calle de Vida in Tierrasanta several exhilarating hours later.

For those who wish to explore the Park in greater depth, purchase a large fold-out map with the hiking, biking and equestrian trails indicated. Not only does it indicate the topography, but much more detail of the water features is included. (However, Lake Murray is not included on this map.) Produced by Sunbelt Publications, this helpful tool is available for purchase at the Visitor and Interpretive Center Gift Shop.

West Fortuna Region

West Fortuna offers the best mountain biking in MTRP, spectacular ocean views on a clear day, as well as birds-eye views of Mission Gorge and the San Diego River from several high points. It feels as though you're a hundred miles from civilization when exploring several of the more remote trails in the canyons of the West Fortuna region and discovering a treasure trove of habitats and wildlife.

The best way to approach this area is from Tierra-santa, but it is also possible to reach the **Fortuna Mtn. Saddle from the Visitor Center** (2.7 miles one way; Category 5 hike).

🚶 Fortuna Mtn. Saddle from Visitor Ctr.

To access the Fortuna Mountain Saddle area from the Visitor Center, begin by walking down the Visitor Center parking lot access driveway and turning right on the Visitor Center Loop Trail. Follow it to the Jackson Drive parking area and down the hill to the San Diego River.

During the summer months, the river sometimes dries to a trickle, thus allowing you to continue directly across. If there's water, and you don't want to wade, simply hike around the left side of the informational kiosk and across the slag dam (of unknown origin).

NOTE: During periodic high water, the river crossing below the Jackson Drive parking area is extremely dangerous and impassable. Do not attempt to cross; instead drive to Tierrasanta for access to the same trails from Clairemont Mesa Blvd.

Low water flow permitting, once you've crossed the dam and a small seasonal pool shortly thereafter, you will climb a steep service road .6 miles to a "Y" intersection. At the "Y" you will see a trail sign, "Colina Dorada and Fortuna Mtns." The left trail heads northwest to Colina Dorada Drive, with access to the Clairemont Mesa Blvd. trailhead—both in Tierrasanta. The right trail heads northeast, providing access to many of the outstanding and challenging vistas in the Park.

These include the Rim Trail, a beautiful single-track trail which follows the rim of Suycott Wash north along the western side of the wash, eventually connecting to a beautifully forested trail providing the north approach (.6 miles) to North Fortuna Mountain's summit.

Another route departs from the Rim Trail to historical Shepherd Pond, then joins with a continuing trail which parallels SR 52, east to the Grasslands in the East Fortuna area. (More on these trails later in this chapter.)

To reach "the Saddle," turn right at the "Y" and walk about 65 paces before turning right again onto a pleasant single track down to Suycott Wash. When you reach the bottom and a "T" intersection, where several live oak trees provide welcome shade, turn left and head north through Suycott Wash until you come to another intersection of trails. Turn right towards the Fortuna Mountain ridge. At one point this track splits into two trails. Stay to the left for an easier route until you reach a junction, where you turn left briefly before turning right for the final climb to the Saddle. Total distance from the Visitor Center is 2.7 miles to this point.

🚶 Fortuna Mtn. Saddle from Tierrasanta

By starting at the Tierrasanta staging area at the end of Clairemont Mesa Blvd., it is possible to reach the Fortuna Mountain Saddle more directly. Begin by crossing the bridge and turning left. Almost immediately turn right onto a "hiker's only" trail that will lead you down through the chaparral to a service road below. Turn left and follow it along the rim of the canyon to a four-way intersection. Head straight across the intersection and down the slope into Suycott Wash. Continue straight across the canyon floor toward the Fortuna Mountain ridge (several trails will branch off of this trail but do not take them.) Further on, this track splits into two trails. Stay to the left for an easier route until you reach a junction where you turn left briefly before turning right for the final climb to the Saddle. The distance from Clairemont Mesa Blvd. to the Saddle is 1.8 miles.

Once you reach the Saddle, you have several choices. You can either head to the **North Fortuna Summit** (0.35 miles from the Saddle with an elevation gain of 402 ft.); or to **South Fortuna Summit** (0.6 miles with an elevation gain of 205 ft.). From **North Fortuna Summit** you can drop down onto the **North Fortuna Loop trail**, which, if you go to the left, will take you to the Shepherd Pond area, a good place to observe wildlife.

Shepherd Pond from Clairemont Mesa Blvd.

Cross bridge and turn left. After .7 miles turn right on a track simply marked "Trail" to reach the Rim Trail. Turn left on the Rim Trail. When you come to a fork, take the track to the right. When you've traveled about 1.3 miles (from CM Blvd.) there will be another junction with the Rim Trail continuing around to the left. Do not take this; instead, you should continue straight down the hill ahead for about .2 mile to the next left-hand turn. Follow the trail over a small hill and down into a gully, before taking another left-hand trail again up and over a hill until you reach the bottom where a dirt track to the right will lead you to Shepherd Pond. At this point you have traveled 2.3 miles from CM Blvd.

This was a watering hole when the area was used to graze sheep; today a variety of animals use it for the same purpose.

This area is a favorite of Park Ranger Casey Smith: "There are few non-native plants in this area and there are lots of birds and wildlife. It's a good place for biologists who have done bat surveys and studied tree frogs in the area. Best of all there aren't too many people that make it to this remote site."

🚶 Suycott Wash/South Fortuna Mtn.

Suycott Wash/South Fortuna Mountain Trail begins just 65 paces from the right hand turn at the "Y" intersection mentioned on page 77. Look for the sign and follow the trail down .4 miles to the bottom of the wash. As you arrive at the bottom and the welcome shade of the numerous oak trees, look on your right for the South Fortuna Trail sign.

This trail (1.2 miles) will follow the creek bed through a continuing oak grove before crossing a small bridge. It will shortly join up with the South Fortuna southerly access trail.

The beginning of the climb, up to a lazy switchback, is fairly easy. But the best is yet to come. The trail gradually increases in steepness to an area where steps have been placed, using a combination of railroad ties, 4 x 4s, and finally rock as you near the top. Count the number of steps...you'll be surprised! You'll agree it's all worth it though.

Take a right turn at the top to the South Fortuna overlook. (The Visitor Center looks pretty small from here!) Now reverse course and take the gradual .4 mile hike up South Fortuna's spine to the summit. You can turn back and retrace here or continue down .6 miles to the Fortuna Saddle and perhaps even tackle the difficult .35 mile trek up the North Fortuna Summit.

🚶 North/South Fortuna Mtns. Loop

North and South Fortuna Summits Loop is a difficult (Category 5) hike which starts at the Saddle, but could just as easily begin at the North or South Fortuna Summit. It includes a loop down through the Suycott Wash, the climb up South Fortuna Mtn. (elev. 1094 ft.) and an easy .6 miles down and back to the Saddle. All together this loop is 4.1 miles with a total descent of 811 feet and a total ascent of 655 ft. Just remember that these numbers are in addition to the effort you made to reach either summit to begin the Loop!

From the Saddle, head up 3.5 miles to the North Fortuna Summit and then, follow a trail down the northerly slope (towards SR52). When you reach the bottom (.6 miles), turn left. Follow a short connector trail for .7 miles and turn left again on the trail to the Suycott Wash turnoff. During this .7 miles, you'll pass two trails connecting to the right with signs to Shepherd Canyon and Shepherd Pond. Ignore them and stay on the trail to Suycott Wash.

INDIAN PAINTBRUSH

A third turn, angling to the right, just .1 miles beond the last, will have a sign for Suycott Wash. Take it and follow it .5 miles down to a fork with one trail leading up the northerly slope and the other one a hard left. Follow the left trail a short distance to the bottom of the wash and then turn right (south) on a single track "hikers-only" trail. Follow this trail .6 miles to the beginning of the climb to South Fortuna's ridge. The climb to the ridge is 550 ft. vertical and .6 miles. The last 250 ft. vertical will be on 358 steps (count 'em) fashioned from 4 x 4 timbers and rocks.

Once at the top of the ridge (elev. 918 ft.), turn right just a few feet to one of the best overlooks in the Park with great views of the MTRP Visitor Center and beyond. Afterward, reverse course and head east on an easy hike (180 ft. gain) up the spine of South Fortuna .4 miles to its summit.

This is a sensitive habitat area so you'll have to stay on trail, but be advised—the vista you left at the overlook is far better!

After an easy .6 miles down from the South Fortuna summit (-205 ft.) to the Fortuna Saddle, you can turn right or left to proceed down the way you came.

🚶 Rim Trail

The best access for the **Rim Trail Loop** (3.1 miles roundtrip is from Clairemont Mesa Blvd. in Tierrasanta. This is a wonderful hiking trail, a favorite of runners, and one of the easier biking trails, providing great views into Suycott Wash and downtown San Diego. Cross bridge and turn left. After a .7 mile medium level climb (218 feet vertical), the loop follows most of the Suycott Wash canyon rim before turning northward, where it intersects with the Portobelo Ridge Trail. Here you have the option of continuing onward around the Rim Trail loop, or following the challenging Ridge Trail, which adds .75 miles and two nasty climbs totaling 384 ft. (combined loop climbs equal 602 ft.).

You might even spot a rare vernal pool in the spring-time; an entire ecosystem comes to life after a few rains. (However if you should be lucky enough to see one, <u>do not disturb</u> the pool as these are very fragile, endangered ecosystems.) Notice the cobblestones along the trail (if you're biking, you're bound to notice!); the rounded stones provide clues to the geological history of this ridge—this whole area except for the tallest peaks was once under the ocean. In fact, according to Park staff, the mountain peaks such as Del Cerro, Mt. Helix and Mt. Miguel that can be glimpsed from MTRP, at one time formed an island arc in a vast sea.

Quarry Loop Trail from Clairemont Mesa Blvd.

This relatively short (2.1 miles roundtrip) loop is one of the most accessible (Category 2) evening "with a view" hiking trails in the Park. From the CM Blvd. parking lot, walk across the bridge. As you turn left up the hill on the main trail, look for a break in the fence and immediately turn right on a narrow (no sign, but it is a hikers-only) trail down across the gully .2 miles to join the service road. Turn right on the service road for a short walk to an inter-section and the Quarry Ridge Trail trailhead.

Follow the reverse switchback to the left .1 miles and 160 ft. vertical to the highest point of the hike (766 ft.). Another tenth of a mile on a gradual descent, you will see a sign pointing to the right—Quarry Ridge Loop. Don't turn onto it, as you'll be returning on it later. Continue down the ridge—now a single track trail—another .2 miles to an overlook on your left with views of the quarry and beyond. On the right is a beautiful landscape of native flora.

Just a short distance beyond, the trail bends northwest, following the rim of a small canyon .3 miles to a "T." Turn right and follow it .1 miles to the westerly junction of Quarry Loop Trail that you didn't follow earlier. Turn right and hike a scenic .2 miles back to the junction with a left turn on the main Quarry Trail that you came up on. This is the conclusion of the loop. So from here, backtrack down to the main trail. As you arrive at the bottom, turn right for a very short distance before taking the left fork in the road—the one you came on. Soon you will turn left again and go up through the gully, left at the top of the trail, and an almost immediate right back to the bridge.

East Fortuna

East Fortuna is the primary horseback riding area of MTRP but it also offers some of the easiest hiking and mountain biking to be found in the Park. This region also offers some of the best bird watching. It is also possible to access some of the more remote, challenging trails from this region.

Very popular with residents of Santee and other East County cities, the trails in East Fortuna are well-used on weekends. Part of the attraction lies in the fact that many of the hikes are suitable for children or older adults because of the gentle grade. At the same time, it contains three of the most important habitats—grasslands, chaparral and riparian ecosystems. Rapidly disappearing from the southwest, the grasslands in MTRP offer a rare glimpse at these habitats preferred by many songbirds and small mammals. Bring along a pair of binoculars and/or a magnifying glass for a productive wildlife trek in this area.

🚶 Grasslands Loop

Trails that you can enjoy in this area include the Grasslands Loop, Oak Canyon and the ascent to the Fortuna Mountain Saddle. Begin your **Grasslands Loop** walk or ride at the low water crossing east of Old Mission Dam and west of Kumeyaay Lake Campground off of the Father Junipero Serra Trail. On this leisurely loop you stroll across a bridge, then up and away from the banks of the San Diego River before the grasslands will come into view. Stop to read the interpretive signs at the Grassland Crossings kiosk, and then go either to the right or the left to complete the loop. Along the way, look for a sign and take a short side-trip to see a great example of Kumeyaay Indian grinding rocks. The 1.2 mile-long Grasslands Loop trail is ranked a Category 1 trail (leisurely) by the Park staff.

🚶 North Fortuna Mtn.

North Fortuna Mountain via the Grasslands Crossing (access from Kumeyaay Lake Campground parking area) is a difficult Category 5 hike, covering 3 miles round trip. Vertical climb is 1198 ft. from the Crossings trailhead. From the parking area, walk a short distance west of the parking lot on Father Junipero Serra Trail to the pipe gate and Grasslands trailhead sign on the right.

Follow the trail across the San Diego River and onto the grasslands.

At the kiosk, take the right-hand trail. After another 100 feet the trail veers left. Look for a sign "Oak Canyon-Fortuna Mountains." Proceed north along this trail, which gradually becomes steeper with one switchback, to a summit and an 18 ft. altitude gain from the river crossing. At this point you will notice a trail junction to the right. Ignore it and proceed straight ahead down and up, following the signs to North Fortuna. This service road leads into Oak Canyon (elev. 412 ft.) and will merge with the Oak Canyon trail. Don't get sidetracked! Continue on the service road and climb 477 ft. and another .6 miles to the Fortuna Mountain Saddle (elev. 889 ft.). The final ascent is very steep—in fact the last 300 paces are known as "The Wall."

To reach the summit of North Fortuna, turn north from the saddle and climb the short .35 mile, 402 ft. climb to the summit, which at 1291 ft. is the 3rd highest peak in the Park. As is true of all the peaks, North Fortuna offers great views in all directions. Wedged into the rocks at the top, is a coffee can with notes from previous hikers as well as a note and pen from your author (CR). So please log in and leave your impressions.

(Hint: There are actually three peaks on North Fortuna. The others are a few feet less in elevation and within a few hundred yards along the ridge trail to the northwest. We've been told that the 3rd peak is a great spot to watch the Navy's Blue Angels aerobatic team during the annual Miramar Air Show.)

🚶 Fortuna Mtn. Saddle from Mast Blvd.

Fortuna Mountain Saddle Trail from Mast Blvd. offers a challenging hike or bike ride with a great deal of variety. Begin your visit to the Park at the end of the paved road. Mast Blvd. is the main equestrian entrance to the Park, but there is usually plenty of street parking available for hikers and mountain-bikers. Additional parking and picnic facilities will be added at this entrance in the near future.

From Mast Blvd. you will first pass through the grasslands, following the signs to Fortuna Mountain. You will eventually find yourself on a rutted service road that crosses the Oak Canyon trail and continues west to the Fortuna Saddle. Along the way you'll have great views into the sage scrub and chaparral habitats that dominate the hillsides. If you're biking, beware of deep ruts in places, and horses and riders who sometimes share the trail. Ride blind curves very carefully, especially on the descent. Continue to follow signs to the crest of the Saddle. The last 300 paces are the most difficult—in fact this feature is commonly referred to as "The Wall."

🚶 Fortuna Mtn. Loop

From the Saddle you can continue to the summit of North Fortuna (see previous hike description), do a loop that includes North and South Fortuna (see page 81), or access several more trails in the West Fortuna region (pages 76-84).

Kumeyaay Lake and Campground

Kumeyaay Lake and Campground are also situated in the East Fortuna region of the Park. The habitat along the shores of lakes and seasonal ponds displays riparian species as well as plants adapted to marshes. Cattails, bulrushes and other moisture dependent plants attract an array of birds, insects and other animals not found elsewhere in the Park. Kumeyaay Lake, a man-made lake fed by the San Diego River on the site of an old gravel mining pit, is home to a number of fish species as well as migratory waterfowl.

After mining operations ceased in the 1960s, a group of senior citizens lobbied the city to obtain temporary use of the Lake for fishing, hiking and picnicking. They also hoped to create a sanctuary for small animals and migratory birds. The group then diligently cleared the brush and stocked the lake with fish. They named the water feature "Hollins Lake," after one of their members who spearheaded the effort.

An old newspaper clipping about the seniors' project detailed future plans to include "over-night camping and expanded outdoor activities…" They most certainly would be pleased with current uses of the area today, which are consistent with that early vision.

In the spring of 2003, Kumeyaay Lake Campground staff member Marla Gilmore said that despite occasional visitors from France, Germany and Switzerland, the campground may well be San Diego's best-kept secret.

"It's an ideal place for families to try camping for the first time, not too far from home. As a City park facility, no alcohol is allowed. We're designed for recreational vehicles as well as tent camping, and allow two tents to be set up on one site. Even single mothers feel safe here…

"Come set up camp, use one of our barbecues to make dinner and roast marshmallows, come to a star party in the amphitheatre, and go to bed early; then take a nature hike in the morning with one of the Park Rangers."

You can also hike at Kumeyaay Lake on your own. The Category 1 trails, which you can access from the Campground, lead to the left or to the right, but they do not connect all the way around the lake because of the sensitive nesting habitat in the area. Covering both of the trails and then back to the campground will equal about a 1 mile hike roundtrip. The views are very peaceful, offering many opportunities to see wildlife close-up.

Marla says Kumeyaay Lake is also a good spot for first-time fishermen to try their hand at the sport. However, the staff advises "catch-and-release," rather than cooking and eating the fish, because the San Diego River is at the bottom of the watershed in this area; everything flows into it.

The convenience and solitude afforded by this unique environment more than makes up for this one drawback. "Besides, if fishing for food is your goal, Lake Murray is only a short drive away—also within Mission Trails Regional Park!" adds Marla.

Mission Gorge Region

Mission Gorge is centrally located in the heart of the Park, is bisected by Father Junipero Serra Trail, and can be accessed by car from both San Diego and from Santee. Geographically speaking, Mission Gorge is the V-shaped outlet carved over millennia by the San Diego River as it made its way to the sea. This is the spectacular location of the Visitor and Interpretive Center, a variety of trails, the best views of the river, and the Old Mission Dam.

For a first visit to the Park, this is the best place to begin. Spend an hour in the Visitor Center learning more about the region, enjoy the great views from both levels of the Center, then pick up a map and an interpretive brochure for a self-guided hike on the Visitor Center Loop, or join a nature walk with a volunteer Trail Guide (offered at 9: 30 a.m. every Wednesday, Saturday and Sunday from the Visitor Center).

Visitor Center Loop

The Visitor Center Loop trail is 1.4 miles round trip and is well-suited for hiking or mountain biking. Moderate in the type of challenge it offers, it is considered a Category 2 trail. But the varieties of wildlife, native plant life and even geology that can be viewed along this route make it an ideal trail to tackle first for those used to doing some hiking or for beginners in good physical condition. Hopefully you picked up that interpretive brochure mentioned above in the Visitor Center that will tell you things to look for along the way. If you have time, follow the signs and take a short side trip to a riverside grinding area used by generations of Kumeyaay Indians. Regardless, at the end of this very pleasant hike, you will have a better appreciation for the precious resources and history contained within Mission Trails Regional Park.

For those serious hikers who have the time and want to continue on, it is also possible to access Suycott Wash and the West Fortuna Region of MTRP from this trail at the Jackson Drive entrance to the Park. **(Note: It will be necessary to ford the San Diego River on this hike. Be prepared to get your shoes and pant legs wet! This is a seasonal crossing—use extreme caution after winter and spring rains and do not proceed if the water is very deep.)**

Father Junipero Serra Trail

There are two spacious parking lots adjacent to the Visitor Center and street parking near the entrance to **Father Junipero Serra Trail** off Mission Gorge Road. It is also possible to drive through this area in a northerly direction at no faster than 15 miles per hour. But if you can walk or bike the 1.8 mile trail in both directions, you will be rewarded with one of the most pleasant experiences in the Park.

Rock climbing and bird watching are two of the primary activities enjoyed in this area. Whether jogging on the paved Father Junipero Serra Trail or hiking to the north side of the dam, keep your eyes peeled for red-tail hawks soaring on the air currents above the gorge and for herons wading in the marshy areas around the dam.

Take a side trip off the Father Junipero Serra Trail to look at the Indian Grinding rocks down by the river's edge.

🚶 Oak Grove Trail

Cool off under the trees along the Oak Grove Trail near the Visitor Center as you watch butterflies and dragonflies darting about in the dappled shade of ancient oaks in a seep area fed by a natural spring. Children and adults will enjoy exploring a replica of a Kumeyaay dwelling constructed here. This easy trail makes a one mile loop. It is considered a Category 1 trail, and can be accessed from two locations along Father Junipero Serra Trail—one across from the driveway leading to the Visitor Center, the other about 0.2 miles north of this driveway, along Father Junipero Serra Trail.

🚶 Oak Canyon Trail

Oak Canyon Trail can be accessed from the Old Mission Dam at the north end of Father Junipero Serra Trail. To access the **Oak Canyon Trail from Old Mission Dam**, follow the walkway west from the Dam, down to the San Diego River. Cross a foot bridge and head north following the signs to Oak Canyon. The trail (1.7 miles one way; Category 3 hike) becomes fairly steep and narrow in places alongside a creek bed, allowing hiking only. At one point this hiking-only trail intersects a service road that leads to Fortuna Mountain. Turn left and follow this road for a short distance (about 60 paces) before turning right and continuing up Oak Canyon through some dramatic boulder-filled scenery toward Highway 52. A seasonal waterfall and Kumeyaay grinding slicks appear a short distance before coming to the Hwy. 52 bridge across Oak Canyon.

Enjoy different scenery and shorten the hike a bit on your return by turning left at the service road and following this road back through the Grasslands to the Old Mission Dam, rather than continuing down the Oak Canyon Trail the way you came. This loop is 3.1

OAK CANYON WATERFALL

miles roundtrip (elevation gain 240 ft.). The wildflowers and water features are especially beautiful along this trail during the early spring.

🚶 Climbers Loop Trail

The **Climbers Loop Trail** is a short, one mile loop that provides access to the climbing areas on the west face of Kwaay Paay. Approximately .21 mile of the loop is a portion of Father Junipero Serra Trail. Both the north and south trails to the base of the climbs are very steep and rough near the top with a connecting lateral trail. This trail was developed to provide access to the climbing area and is not suitable for the casual hiker. This is considered a Category 5 hike—in other words, a very challenging trail. But for those who are up to the challenge, they are rewarded with spectacular views.

🏃 BMX Track / Loop

Several other trails can be accessed north of Mission Gorge Road on this side of the Park. The main entrance to the Park is located between Jackson Drive and Golfcrest Drive on the north side of Mission Gorge Road. But there is also a trailhead and parking lot at the Mission Gorge Road intersection with Jackson Drive, and one a little further west at the intersection with Deerfield Circle. This one will take you into an old quarry site behind the Deerfield Pump Station, where piles of dirt today are fashioned into jump sites for a **BMX (bicycle motocross) Track**. (Note: The track is provided for non-motorized vehicles only.)

BMX bicycle racing has been around since the '60s. Interest in this sport has had its peaks and valleys, but is currently rising to new levels.

A bonus for Park users is a scenic 1.1 mile loop around the BMX site, starting from the Visitor Center. Begin on the Visitor Center Loop Trail just east of the Visitor Center. When you reach the Jackson Drive parking lot, look for the BMX trail sign on the left, just 100 yards past the kiosk as you start down the hill. The trail turns back down following a small creek for about .2 miles to the top of the climb and another info kiosk.

While hiking up this segment, look to the right and view all five of MTRP's peaks—there are only a few places in the Park you can do this. The peaks are, from your right to left: Cowles Mtn., elevation 1591 ft.; Pyles Peak, elevation 1379 ft; Kwaay Paay, elevation 1194 ft.; South Fortuna Mtn., elevation 1094 ft.; and North Fortuna Mtn., elevation 1291 ft.

Once at the top, turn right and go down, passing the viewing area on your left, into the BMX area. If there are "BMXers" practicing or competing, watch from the viewing area. You'll be amazed at how they jump the berms! Continue to follow the trail through the site, up to its rim. Follow the trail beginning west with views of the rock quarry, and then bending around east .4 miles to the creek trail leading back up to your starting point.

🚶 Old Mission Dam

On the Santee side, you'll find an entrance to the Park, just west of West Hills Parkway on the north side of Mission Gorge Road. Follow the signs to the Old Mission Dam where you may park in a lot close to the dam off Father Junipero Serra Trail, or on either side of the road up to the point where the Trail becomes one way going the opposite direction for automobile traffic. There is also an additional lot at the intersection of Bushy Hill Drive and Father Junipero Serra Trail across from the entrance to Kumeyaay Lake Campground.

There are interpretive signs, picnic tables, trash and recycling facilities and portable restroom facilities near the Old Mission Dam. Licensed fishing is allowed in the river by the dam but only from the shore or the dam itself. Staff suggests "catch-and-release" fishing since the San Diego River water quality is affected by run-off from homes and storm drains as it makes it way to the sea. (No swimming or boating is permitted. Should you choose to eat your catch, clean your fish elsewhere as the remains attract many forms of wildlife and disrupt their normal feeding pattern.)

Kwaay Paay

From this side of the Mission Gorge area of the Park, you will find the easiest access to the dam—great for those who can't walk very far. But if you're looking for more active recreation, you can easily find trails here that will take you to the top of **Kwaay Paay** peak (1,194 ft.) for a vigorous hike. A very steep trail up to the ridge of Kwaay Paay (meaning "Chieftan or Leader" in the Kumeyaay language) is arguably the most difficult one to hike in the Park, even though it's only the fourth highest peak. This 1.2 mile hike (category 5) is quite steep in places, with a total elevation gain of 880 feet. Then once you "summit," there's really not much to see. The trail ends where you encounter an off-limits sensitive habitat area. But it's a super workout. And as you climb (and descend), there are some spectacular views of the campground, grasslands and beyond.

You can access the trail to the top of Kwaay Paay from two locations: the parking lot at the intersection of Bushy Hill Dr. and Father Junipero Serra Trail, or from the southeast side of Father Serra Trail, near the Old Mission Dam—where a more forgiving trail begins.

NOTE: It is highly recommended that you wear trail running shoes or hiking boots with good tread. Much of the Kwaay Paay trail is solid granite covered with decomposed granite granules. Hiking sticks— either single or double—are also recommended.

Cowles Mountain Area

Cowles Mountain and Pyles Peak represent the two highest points in MTRP, and Cowles Mountain's primary hiking trail, up the steep face of the mountain near the intersection of Navajo and Golfcrest Dr., is the most widely used trail in the Park. On a clear day the views from the top are unparalled, while the climb itself is athletically challenging.

What's in a Name?

The mountain is named for George A. Cowles (pronounced "cōals"), a wealthy gentleman from the East who made his fortune in the cotton business, later settling in California as a fruit, horse and cattle rancher. He owned over six square miles of land in the El Cajon valley, and became known as the "raisin king of the U.S." before his death in 1887. Three years later his wife married a local real estate developer named Milton Santee. Cowlestown became "Santee" in 1893, while the town's first school became Santee School. The historical name of Cowles Mountain nearly disappeared as well, until it became a part of MTRP.

Climbing Cowles Mountain for the view from the top was a favorite local pastime for generations. And for 40 years, from 1931 to 1971, San Diego State College freshman classes painted and repainted an "S" (for San Diego State) on the southwest side of the mountain.

In 1974, the mountain was acquired for park purposes by the City of San Diego after several concerned citizens and elected officials pursued its purchase to prevent further development of the land. The price required from the City and the County was only $2.2 million, provided the deal could close by the end of the year. A loan from the County made the purchase possible, approved in an "11th hour" vote by three out of the five members of the County Board of Supervisors on December 31, 1974.

🚶 Hiking the Highest Peaks in San Diego

Cowles Mtn. is by far the most popular (and populated) trail in San Diego County. It has become a fitness playground for all ages. Its popularity is regularly substantiated by the high number of hikers/joggers/runners on the trail at any time. In fact, between 30 minutes before sunrise to 30 minutes past in the evening, upwards of 800 per day enjoy this difficult and scenic hike. But unlike other trails, nearly everyone says "hi" and even more importantly, looks out for other people.

There are five ways to access Cowles Mountain and Pyles Peak. Each offers its own challenges and opportunities. Most people currently use the trail that can be accessed from the intersection of Golfcrest and Navajo

Road. This steep trail leads to the top of one of the highest points in the City of San Diego (1,591 ft.) for an excellent 360 degree view. (The elevation gain is 966 ft.) At the top are large painted graphics depicting the landmarks one can see from this vantage point. Large natural boulders scattered around the summit provide good places to sit and rest while enjoying the view. In case you're wondering, the antennae that are attached to the crest of the hill nearby generate annual lease fees, providing funds for capital improvements and land acquisition for MTRP.

From Golfcrest & Navajo — Starting from an attractive staging area with parking and restrooms at the base of the mountain, the trail is 1.5 miles one way with many switchbacks, and is one of the most challenging in the Park.

Because of the trail's fairly consistent rate of altitude gain, many older people and others who have made a commitment to health and fitness a priority, have found that even a slow beginning walk to the first switchback and back is a good start and yields a great feeling of accomplishment. Very gradually increasing distance on a regular basis is of extreme importance and could fulfill a realistic goal of someday touching the plaque on the rock at the top.

The trail is also a favorite of families, especially those with young children introducing them to hiking. It is rare that you ascend the trail without seeing young children— some in backpack carriers, some running, and some "huffing and puffing"—with huge smiles on their faces.

Climbing Data/Altitude Gain

.25 mile	160'
.5 mile	323'
.75 mile	1152'
1 mile	1302'
1.25 mile	1413'
1.5 miles	1591'

From Barker Way — For safety reasons bicycles are not allowed on the Golfcrest/Navajo trail, but are permitted on an access road from Barker Way. The elevation gain on the access road is less (870 ft.), but the trail is longer (1.6 miles one way). The trail to the top of Cowles Mountain along the access road is considered to be moderately challenging. There is a more challenging hike that can also be accessed **from the Barker Way Service Road**, through the chaparral and up the east-facing side of the mountain.

This trail starts out on a service road off Barker Way. After about 200 paces, keep an eye out on your left for the trailhead sign. Hike up the multi-switchback trail .85 miles to its intersection with Cowles Mountain's main trail. Follow the Cowles Mtn. trail .44 miles to the summit. To reach Barker Way, turn north from Navajo Road onto Cowles Mountain Blvd., left on Boulder Lake Drive and right on Barker Way. You'll see the trailhead and pipe gate about a half block down on the left. As you park on this quiet residential street, be aware and considerate of the neighbors. This trek nearly equals the rigors of the hike on the other side with one major advantage—lack of people. However, near the summit, because this trail joins the trail from the Golfcrest staging area, it will be bustling on a busy weekend day.

From Big Rock Road in Santee — To ascend to the top of **Cowles Mountain from Big Rock Road** in Santee, follow a picturesque trail that meanders through chaparral-covered foothills before making the final steep ascent. (The total elevation gain on this trail is 1,150 feet.) After .1 miles, turn right at an intersection. Hike over many railroad ties for 1.5 miles to a service road. Turn right on service road for .9 miles to Cowles summit. (Total mileage is 2.5 miles.) Although longer than the other trails that ascend Cowles Mountain, this trail is not frequently used and provides an opportunity for a more reflective hike and frequent wildlife sightings. Big Rock Road can be accessed off Mission Gorge Road; follow it to the top and park in the cul-de-sac. Be considerate of the residents in this peaceful neighborhood.

From Mesa Road in Santee — Finally, one can reach the summit of **Cowles Mountain from Mesa Road**, also in Santee. This trail joins the trail from Big Rock Park about .5 miles from the top. The elevation gain and the length are the same; both trails from Santee are quite challenging but very rewarding. To reach the trailhead, turn on Mesa Road off Mission Gorge Road and drive past Chet Herritt School and Big Rock Park to an open gate and continue .3 miles beyond to a parking area where you'll see a kiosk. The first segment of this trail meanders through some of the best of the chaparral. The trail intersects with the Big Rock trail at mile .7, and then up .5 miles to the service road and turn right .9 miles to the summit.

From Cowles Mtn. to Pyles Peak — A free map in the Visitor Center describes the **hike from Cowles Mountain summit to Pyles Peak** as "difficult with a minus 210 ft. elevation change." This statement is reasonably accurate, i.e., Pyle's Peak's summit is 216 feet below Cowles Mountain summit, and is in fact a difficult and challenging hike, but as you will soon discover, the ups and downs of this beautiful trail equate to much more than 216 ft!

The trail begins at the top of Cowles Mountain, just a hundred feet short of the summit marker. A left turn down some steps to the north followed by another left turn onto a service road, leads to the Pyles Peak trailhead. The first .5 miles drops through five switchbacks into a ravine, bottoming at 1257 ft. with a total descent of -334 ft. This is followed by a climb ending in six switchbacks (1372 ft.) with an altitude gain of +115 ft.

Along this ridge, a sign directs you east on an optional side trip that take you .4 miles up (44 ft. vertical) to a viewpoint overlooking the East County. At 1416 ft. it is 44 ft. higher than Pyles Peak!

Back down to the main trail, a gradual descent leads into a shallow ravine (-45 ft.) and after a small rise, is followed by yet another descent (-185 ft.) ending at an overlook with great views of the MTRP Visitor Center, downtown San Diego and on clear days, from Mexico to North County. It is from here that the "assault of the summit begins." The trail follows a more or less straight line east up a steep .35 mile climb (226 ft. vertical) to Pyles Peak's 1379 ft. summit. You will see a large chunk of granite which marks the top. Congratulations, you've done it!

NOTE: When planning this hike, one must take into account that the only access to the Pyles Peak trail is via Cowles Mountain summit, requiring a 1.5 mile, 966 ft. climb (and descent) before and after the Pyles Peak hike. This results in a total distance of nearly 6 miles and a total ascent (and descent) of over 1,900 ft.

Lake Murray Region

Lake Murray offers a welcome respite from everyday stress by providing an opportunity to walk, jog, bike, boat or fish in a very peaceful setting. Tucked in the midst of a suburban neighborhood, Lake Murray is actually a fresh water reservoir owned by the City of San Diego, serving as a primary water source for over 400,000 local residents. Its origins date back to 1895, when the San Diego Flume Company built a small, earthen and rock-paved structure to dam up a small creek running through Alvarado Canyon. They called it the La Mesa Dam.

History of Lake Murray

By 1918, the company that then owned it, the Cuyamaca Water Company, decided to build a larger structure and constructed a multiple arch concrete dam, 117 feet tall and 870 feet long just downstream of the La Mesa Dam. It was dedicated in 1918 and named for James Murray, a water resources entrepreneur and co-owner of the Cuyamaca Water Company. In 1926, the company sold its holdings to an East County publicly held irrigation trust, now known as Helix Water District; in 1961 they granted ownership of Murray Dam and its reservoir to the City of San Diego.

In 1950, the City of San Diego built the Alvarado Water Filtration Plant adjacent to Lake Murray. The original capacity of the filtration plant was 60 million gallons per day, which was later expanded to 120 million gallons in the early 1970s. Lake Murray provides water to the Alvarado Water Filtration Plant, which processes and delivers drinking water to more than 400,000 San Diegans.

The City is in the process of upgrading and expanding the Filtration Plant to meet new state and federal regulations, to keep pace with San Diego's increasing demand for water, and to replace equipment that was installed more than 40 years ago. This eight-phase upgrade and expansion project began in 1993 and is scheduled to be completed by 2010.

Fishing and Boating

When full, the reservoir has 171.1 surface acres and a maximum depth of 95 feet. Surrounding the lake are areas of chaparral, grassland and riparian habitat. Its natural beauty and attraction to wildlife have been enjoyed by generations of families since the early 1900s when fishing and duck hunting were popular activities. Although hunting was banned in the 60s, fishing is still very popular. The lake is well stocked with a variety of fish and some record catches have been made there.

The largest fish caught in Lake Murray was a channel catfish caught in 1968, weighing 29 1/2 lbs. In 1992, a carp, weighing 20 lbs., 4 oz., was landed, while more recently a large-mouth bass weighing 18.55 lbs. was hooked in December 2000. Other fish varieties include bluegill, red-ear sunfish, black crappie, yellow bullhead, and whitewater rainbow trout. In fact, each year from November to May, 1200 lbs of rainbow trout fingerlings are stocked weekly in

Lake Murray! The largest one caught to date was a 12 pounder in 1993.

Boating and fishing take place on Wednesdays, Saturdays, Sundays and certain holidays from sunrise to sunset (most years) between November 1 and Labor Day. This schedule is subject to change. For the most current information check the Web site listed on page 106. Privately owned small boats and kayaks are welcome. Certain times of the year fishing classes and tournaments are conducted by city staff. Concession services include rental of outboard motors, row boats, and canoes on a first-come, first-served basis. State fishing licenses can also be purchased. **(Note: Dogs are not allowed on boats–private or rental).**

Fish limits are five trout, five bass, five catfish and 25 crappie, with no limit on other species. Minimum size limit for bass is 12 inches. Fish catch information is updated weekly and can be found on a good Web site: *www.sannet.gov/water/recreation/murray.shtml* .

The fishing and boating facilities have recently undergone a $700,000 upgrade and now feature a two-lane launch ramp, courtesy dock and restrooms. Other improvements enjoyed by all visitors to Lake Murray include new landscaping and resurfacing of the well-used parking lot.

🏃 Hiking/Biking Around the Lake

A paved hiking/biking path almost circles the lake for 3.2 miles from the entrance near Kiowa Drive in La Mesa to the dam's gates in San Diego. While it's not possible to do a complete circuit around the lake, hundreds of people utilize the path for daily exercise routines and receive a vigorous workout by making a roundtrip to the gates and back. The grade is essentially flat with a few very gentle inclines so it is frequently shared by Rollerbladers® and young families teaching their little ones to bike ride or skate.

This necessitates some sensible and courteous "rules of the road:" Walk, jog, skate or ride no more than two abreast; stay to the right and allow faster traffic to pass on the left. Dogs must be kept on a leash at all times and at least 50 feet away from the water.

For safety purposes, there is now signage identifying the names of the coves and points of land passed along the path. If you or a companion needs to call the paramedics for any reason, be sure to name the closest landmark for faster assistance.

Above all, take the time to look around and appreciate your surroundings. According to Barbara Anderson, president of the Friends of Lake Murray, who jogs at the Lake almost daily, many people walk or run with their heads down or are too busy talking with a companion to notice the pair of osprey she has seen fishing and building a nest, or the raccoon parents teaching their baby how to fish. She has seen coyotes, barn owls, a great horned owl, white pelicans, many turtles and most exciting of all, a peregrine falcon.

The Lake Murray Path can be accessed from the parking lot at the Kiowa Drive entrance, from a path off of Baltimore Drive, where street parking is permitted, and from Murray Park Drive (Golfcrest heading south off Navajo Road becomes Murray Park Drive; Park entrance will be on left-hand side).

Picnicking Facilities

Picnicking is a popular activity at Lake Murray year-round. There are 10 barbecues and 64 picnic tables located around the lake. Patrons can also bring their own barbecues for use in designated areas only. However, no ground fires or glass containers are allowed. And, as is the rule throughout the rest of Mission Trails Regional Park, the consumption of alcoholic beverages is prohibited.

There is a lovely area for a quiet picnic on a hillside overlooking the Lake which can be accessed from the end of Dwayne Avenue in a residential neighborhood. It is okay to park on the city streets but please be considerate of the residents. Likewise if you decide to have a picnic in this area, be sure to remove all trash when you leave. You may not find trash containers handy so be prepared with a trash bag you can take in the car with you.

Other Recreational Opportunities

Additional recreational facilities for public use are available at **Lake Murray Community Park**. These include a neighborhood pocket park with picnic facilities, and Little League and soccer fields at the north end of the reservoir, accessible from Murray Park Drive. The **Lake Murray Tennis Club** (7051 Murray Park Drive) is part of this complex and includes 10 beautiful city-owned courts. Club amenities include a clubhouse with restrooms and shower facilities and a Pro Shop. These have a separate entrance and parking off of Murray Park Drive, which can be accessed at the intersection of Madra Drive and Park Ridge Blvd., just past the neighborhood park mentioned above.

Court usage is obtained through reservations made by phone to the clubhouse (619) 469-3232, or in person at the clubhouse. Use of the tennis courts is free to club members and available to the general public for a small daily fee. Club members pay an annual membership fee. The Club also participates in various tennis leagues, holds in-house tournaments, and has periodic social activities. Teaching professionals are available for individual and group lessons.

Mission Trails Golf Course (7380 Golfcrest Place) is an 18-hole championship course within MTRP. The 6,000-

yard, par 71 course is located between Cowles Mountain and Lake Murray and offers panoramic views of both. The first nine holes are nestled in the valley between the two geographical features, while the back nine meander along the shores of Lake Murray. The Course offers cart rentals, a driving range, annual golf tournaments, a Nike Golf Learning Center, and full-day and half-day junior golf camps. There is a restaurant and lounge with kitchen and banquet facilities available.

PGA professionals staff the Course which is leased from the City of San Diego and managed by the American Golf Corporation. For tee times and other information, call (619) 460-5400. Limited information is available on the Web site *www.americangolf.com*. Once you open the site, search for Mission Trails Golf Course by region or zip code (92119).

The clubhouse is located near the intersection of Golfcrest Place and Navajo Road, near the Golfcrest staging area for Cowles Mountain.

Lake Murray is open for general recreation (walking, picnicking, etc.) seven days a week, year-round. Additional information is available on the City of San Diego Web site, ci.san-diego.ca.us/water/recreation, or by calling the concessionaire at (619) 390-0223.

Best areas for each type of activity

There is almost no end to the choices one could make planning an outing in Mission Trails Regional Park. But depending on your mood, how much time you have, your physical strength and sports equipment available, there may be certain factors that will influence what part you decide to visit. Following is a general guide to different activities as well as suggested places within the Park in which to enjoy them.

Visiting with Children

Visitors will see children—even very young children —in many different places in MTRP, sometimes hiking up the steepest trails with their chaperones. But for caretakers who are not so ambitious, there are several great places to introduce a child to the wealth of experiences that await them.

The Visitor and Interpretive Center offers films, inter-active exhibits and even children's nature books to peruse in the library. A foot path leading to the Center entrance is lined with animal sound exhibits guaranteed to delight little ones. Older children will appreciate exploring the native plant identification garden adjacent to the center (ask for an interpretive brochure inside), following a self-guided tour of the Visitor Center Loop trail (ask for tour brochure) or joining a nature walk with a knowledgeable Trail Guide (offered frequently, especially on weekends).

A walk along the nearby Oak Grove trail is suitable for strollers, and offers enough variety to keep a child's interest. Some of the things they might observe include unusual birds, small mammals, dragonflies and spider webs. Underneath the shady oaks, there's even a replica of a Kumeyaay shelter ("Ewaa") that children can explore.

Many children have their first introduction to Mission Trails Regional Park at Lake Murray. Picnicking and feeding the ducks are special favorites with the toddler crowd. (This is the only place in the Park where you are allowed to feed the wildlife.) Food dispensers are regularly stocked by "Friends of Lake Murray." Tip: Keep a look out for a special pair of swans named "George" and "Gracie."

LEAST BELL'S VIREOS

Generations of kids have also learned to canoe, ride bikes, roller skate, fish and bird-watch in and around this sparkling reservoir. Many children experience their first extended bike ride on the paved Lake Murray Path. A complete round-trip to the dam gates and back is 6.4 miles. **(Note: There is a great deal of foot, skate and bike traffic at peak times; don't let a child ride too far ahead or behind you if they are not very experienced. Also teach them early on about the importance of moving to the right to let faster traffic pass on the left.)**

Lake Murray is a great place to fish for all ages. Since this is a regularly stocked reservoir, the chances of actually catching something are pretty good; and, because it is a clean reservoir, the fish are quite safe to eat. For older children, there are fishing lessons and junior fishing tournaments offered at different times of the year.

At the north end of the lake are well-used athletic fields and 10 public tennis courts with junior activities as well. If your clan lives near the Lake, consider becoming involved as a family in monthly "Friends of the Lake" volunteer activities like collecting old fishing lines and picking up trash.

Tent camping at Kumeyaay Lake Campground and attending a campfire talk or stargazing party in the amphitheater adjacent to the Lake are popular family activities, and highly recommended for all ages.

From the campground you can walk to the Old Mission Dam, let the kids try their hands at fishing in the lake, or go on a fairly easy bike ride through the Grasslands. Log onto the Web site, *www.mtrp.org*, to reserve a camp site, find out about special classes, walks and volunteer opportunities for different age groups.

Rest and Reflection

Some days one simply wants to be alone in a peaceful setting to shed the stresses of an increasingly technological world or just to get in touch with inner thoughts. Mission Trails Regional Park provides many ideal locations for such a retreat, with the added bonus of natural surroundings and rare glimpses of wildlife close to an urban center.

Obviously the fewer people that share the space, the more peaceful it will be. Therefore avoid the busier spots such as the Cowles Mountain Hiking Trail from the

Navajo and Golfcrest staging area. Instead use one of the less well-traveled paths on the east or north side of the mountain, from Barker Way in San Carlos or Mesa Road or Big Rock Road in Santee. If you reach the summit on a weekend day, you will encounter large numbers of people. Take the time to hike a bit further and rest on an overlook near Pyles Peak before descending the mountain.

Likewise, Lake Murray is enjoyed by as many as 3,000 people a day by some estimates. But there are off-the-beaten path spots where you can contemplate the reservoir from a different vantage point. Park in one of the quiet neighborhoods of Del Cerro and just sit and enjoy the view over the lake to the mountains beyond.

Old Mission Dam is a peaceful spot but can be crowded on a beautiful day. Try crossing the river on the bridge just west of the dam and hiking to the north side. There are several expansive oak trees along the way, offering a quiet resting place in the shade.

Or take the path off Father Junipero Serra Trail that leads to the Grinding Rocks by the San Diego River. Ancient boulders provide comfortable seating to contemplate the river rushing by after a recent rain storm or trickling past in the heat of late summer. Try to imagine Kumeyaay women and children using the rock bed and specially shaped stones to process acorns from the nearby trees into meal.

If you can visit on a weekday, use the Oak Grove Loop trail, find a bench in the shade, and wait and watch for the birds, insects and small mammals that inhabit this lush grove. Or spend a rainy afternoon in the Resource Library at the Visitor and Interpretive Center. The Visitor Center, with its floor to ceiling windows, takes advantage of an awe-inspiring view into the Gorge where the San Diego River passes through.

In the West Fortuna area, from Clairemont Mesa Blvd., hike across the canyon valley to the Rim Trail and down into Suycott Wash. A grove of oak trees and picnic tables will reward your efforts. Explore this valley or simply sit or lean back on one of the benches, looking up through the trees.

For one of the most spectacular views in the Park, with almost no one around, cross Suycott Wash and ascend to the top of South Fortuna Mountain on a steep stairway carved into the mountainside. Or ride a mountain bike on the North Fortuna Loop Trail to Shepherd Pond. Although background freeway noise is ever present (consider it "urban surf" if you will), you'll most likely have this area to yourself for some great wildlife viewing. Bring your binoculars.

Walking, Jogging and Rollerblading®

Many folks walk briskly or jog along trails throughout MTRP, but there are two places that especially lend themselves to this activity because they are paved, well-marked and provide a measured route for daily or weekly exercise routines.

Father Junipero Serra Trail starts and ends at Mission Gorge Road and roughly traces the route of the San Diego River through the Gorge. The Trail is 1.8 miles in length from the Visitor Center to the Old Mission Dam, and automobile traffic (which is allowed to drive at 15 mph in one direction only) is separated from pedestrian, biking and in-line skating traffic by an asphalt berm. There are great views (and sounds) of the river, riparian habitat, and nearby cliffs where raptors nest. This route provides more variety and change in elevation than the second choice.

Lake Murray Path is a gentle, paved road, closed off to any motorized traffic. It is shared by bikers, joggers, walkers, and kids learning to roller skate. This can be a chaotic mix, but plan a visit on a weekday or any day in the early morning or evening, and you'll be rewarded with the peaceful views and sounds of migratory waterfowl and fishing boats or kayaks exploring the coves and bays as you travel along the 3.2 mile trail.

Hiking and Biking

More trails are designated for hiking and biking in Mission Trails Regional Park than any other type of activity. And these trails are found throughout all regions of the Park. In general, the most challenging ones can be found on and around Cowles Mountain and in the West Fortuna region, while more moderate trails are located in the Mission Gorge, East Fortuna and Lake Murray areas.

The best mountain biking, according to Park staff, is accessed from the Calle de Vida or Clairemont Mesa Blvd. trailheads in Tierrasanta. This is the gateway to the Rim Trail, Suycott Wash, the Fortuna Mountain Saddle and North and South Fortuna Mountain. However, it is also possible to access these areas from the Jackson Drive trailhead near the Visitor Center, from the Grasslands Loop near the Kuymeyaay Lake Campground, or from Mast Blvd. in Santee.

Hiking is allowed on 40 miles of designated trails and in every region of the Park. Pick up a comprehensive trail map at the Gift Shop in the Visitor Center, where you can also purchase a California field guide, bird identification resources, and/or wildflower brochure to enhance your hiking experience.

Horseback Riding

In the near future, an Equestrian Staging Area will be opened near the Mast Blvd. entrance to MTRP. In the meantime, this is still the best way to bring your horse into the Park, parking your towing vehicle and trailer along the street. A map showing the horseback riding trails is posted at the trailhead. Most are located in the Grasslands area of the East Fortuna region.

Until the Equestrian Staging Area is complete, a possible alternative is to park your vehicle and trailer in the parking lot at Bushy Hill Drive (across from the entrance to the Kumeyaay Lake Campground) and proceed west along

Father Junipero Serra Trail to a gate and narrow bridge on the right that will take you across the river, and up to the Grasslands Crossing on the other side. However, be aware that this alternate route involves sharing the road with automobile and heavy mountain-biking traffic.

Rock Climbing

There is only one area designated for this activity in MTRP: the sheer granite face of Kwaay Paay Mountain. According to Park staff, there are both aided and unaided (technical) climbs available. The quality of the experience is such that many local climbers prepare for climbing in Yosemite National Park by training on the face of Kwaay Paay. The Climbers Loop trail which intersects Father Junipero Serra Trail in two places, ascends to the base of the cliff through some pretty steep and challenging territory (affectionately called "Middle Earth," by the climbers). Climbing should never be attempted by anyone inexperienced or untrained in the sport, while proper equipment and techniques must always be used by those who tackle the mountain. For more information about the sport and where to learn the proper techniques for climbing, contact San Diego Climbers Coalition or log on to *www.giantsoftware.com/sdcc/*.

Best Places to Picnic

Unwrapping a peanut butter sandwich and enjoying a piece of fruit with the view from the top of North Fortuna Mountain may be the best "picnic" you've ever had, but if, instead, the word "picnic" brings to mind checkered table cloths, thermoses and large coolers packed with chilled food, then you'll be glad to know about the following facilities.

Picnic tables and nearby trash containers are available in six locations within MTRP: Lake Murray, Clairemont Mesa Blvd. in Tierrasanta, Suycott Wash, Kumeyaay Lake Campground, and at the Old Mission Dam. There are also eight tables on a small hill overlooking Mission Gorge behind the Visitor Center.

Lake Murray offers the most extensive picnic facilities with 64 tables and 10 grills. Patrons can also bring their own barbecues for use in designated areas only. However, no ground fires or glass containers are allowed. And as is the rule throughout the rest of Mission Trails Regional Park, the consumption of alcoholic beverages is prohibited at Lake Murray.

Benches are located near the main parking lot and at various points along the 3.2 mile path around the reservoir. Restrooms and running water are available near the concession stand. The Visitor Center also has restrooms running water and picnic tables. Old Mission Dam has several picnic tables, portable restrooms and a drinking fountain. Of particular note in this region of the Park is the Kumeyaay Lake Campground. There are ample parking spots and picnic tables for day use, more picnic tables and grills at each campsite (only available if the campsite is not reserved) and – best of all – a covered pavilion for larger gatherings overlooking the lake.

Coming soon will be another picnic area at the new Equestrian Staging Area. This site will offer picnic tables, grills, portable restrooms and water as well as off-street parking. These facilities will be located near the Mast Blvd. entrance to MTRP in the East Fortuna region.

The West Fortuna region has two great picnic areas, one near the trailhead at Clairemont Mesa Blvd., and one in Suycott Wash. These only have picnic benches and trash containers at the present time but, offer a different visual experience from the other sites .

The author's favorite picnic location is the Grinding Rocks accessed off of the Visitor Center Loop Trail or Father Junipero Serra Trail. No picnic table or restrooms, but great boulders and shade at the river's edge.

No matter where you choose to picnic, remember to remove all trash, dispose of coals (where grills are allowed) in designated containers—and as tempting as it may be— don't feed the wild animals.

Fishing and Boating

Lake Murray is the prime location within MTRP for this activity. The fresh-water reservoir is stocked weekly (November through April) with fish. There are boat ramps, a boat dock with boat and canoe rentals, a concession selling bait and licenses, fishing tournaments and even lessons offered. Shore fishing is allowed at the Old Mission Dam, Kumeyaay Lake, and wherever designated trails intersect the San Diego River. A fishing license is required in all areas for anyone over age 16, and there are limits on minimum size and number (by species) that can be caught in a day. This and other available information, including a history of recent catches at Lake Murray can be found on their Web site: *http://ci.san-diego.ca.us/water/recreation* .

Camping/Kumeyaay Lake Campground

Camping is allowed in only one location within Mission Trails Regional Park, but fortunately offers excellent facilities.

Kumeyaay Lake Campground, adjacent to the lake, with plenty of campsites available for tent camping, offers an individual back-country experience within eight miles of a large urban center! Ranger staff and volunteers also conduct nature hikes for groups and monthly star-gazing parties when skies are clear.

Campers have their choice of 46 primitive (no water or electricity) sites for tents or recreational vehicles. Each site contains picnic and food preparation tables, a fire box, tent pad, and parking space with water. Bathrooms and hot showers are provided nearby. For reservations call (619) 668-2748 or on the Internet at *www.mtrp.org*. The campground is open for entry 9:00 am to 9:00 pm Thursdays through Mondays; the facility is closed on Tuesdays and Wednesdays. More details and photos are available on the Web site listed above.

*COAST
HORNED LIZARD*

CHAPTER 6

Special Opportunities in Mission Trails Regional Park

Become an MTRP volunteer — Volunteers are involved in almost every aspect of managing MTRP—from clearing trails to guiding nature walks, from running the gift shop and greeting visitors to "staffing" the campground entry station. Volunteers provide a vital service while learning more and enjoying this open space jewel.

Organized groups such as scout troops, fraternal organizations, church groups or service clubs are welcome to volunteer on a one-time or regular basis within MTRP. But arrangements must be made in advance with Center staff.

Call (619) 668-3278 or e-mail mtrp@mtrp.org for more info about the many volunteer opportunities available.

Rent the Visitor Center* — This unique and beautiful venue is available for meetings and other events for corporate and non-profit organizations. Enjoy a reception on the patio overlooking dramatic Mission Gorge or hold an educational event in the well-equipped class rooms. *Please note, some restrictions apply. The Visitor Center is not available for commercial use or private functions such as birthday parties, weddings, baptisms, and memorial services. Call Foundation staff, (619) 582-7800, or e-mail mtrp@mtrp.org for more details.

Take a free, guided nature hike — Year-round at 9:30 a.m., on Wednesdays, Saturdays and Sundays, volunteer Trail Guides lead walks that start from the Visitor & Interpretive Center. Explore and learn about the wonders of nature and the people who once lived on this land. Open to the public with no reservations required. Leader will accommodate the physical or special needs of the group.

Occasionally, volunteer Trail Guides also offer interpreted hikes around Kumeyaay Lake Campground or the Old Mission Dam. These hikes will begin at the Campground entry station.

Or join a Park Ranger or another expert to learn more about native plants, Indian lore or wildlife tracking during special programs offered on a regular basis. Wear sturdy shoes and bring water. A hat and sunscreen are recommended. Call the Visitor Center (619) 668-3275, or check the events calendar on the Web site *www.mtrp.org* to find out more about these great free programs.

Educational programs for kids — Guided field trip programs can be arranged during the school year for different grade levels. Emphasis varies depending on age and curriculum guidelines. Call Education Ranger staff at (619) 668-3279 or check the details on the Web site *www.mtrp.org/fieldtrips*.

Also offered are arts and crafts activities, photography classes, campfire programs, and even "Saturday at the Movies" (nature videos).

You can also enroll your child in half-day nature camps. These hands-on programs are offered on a one-day or several day bases on weekends or during school holidays. Some fees may apply, but financial assistance is available. For more information call (619) 668-3275 or log on to *www.mtrp.org*.

Monthly star parties — On the second Friday of every month, join the San Diego Astronomy Association for monthly star parties in the parking lot to the east of the Kumeyaay Lake Campground, for public viewing through the member's telescopes. Members will gather around sunset with their equipment, and remain set up until approximately 10:00 pm., or whenever the crowd disperses. Other opportunities for star-gazing may be offered each month. Check the Park events calendar on the Web at *www.mtrp.org* .

Calling all amateur photographers! Kids and adults compete to take the best photos each year for cash prizes in the Mission Trails photo contest. All photos must be shot within the Park, but any photos that are taken "off-trail" are disqualified. Categories include color and black and white, youth and adult, scenic and flora and fauna. There is an entry fee. Entries are due in May; winners are announced in June. Winning photos are displayed at the Visitor and Interpretive Center. For more details or an entry form, log onto *www.mtrp.org*.

Research Library open to public — For inspiration, not only from the many resources available, but from the view out the windows overlooking Kwaay Paay and the other craggy peaks framing Mission Gorge, spend some quality time alone or with your children in the Research Library at the Visitor & Interpretive Center. You'll find books and periodicals here on topics like geology, history, flora and fauna, archaeology, and paleontology (not just within MTRP, but with an emphasis on Southern California) to satisfy every interest level. Comfy chairs, a computer with links to the Park's Web site, and even a working fireplace for chilly days make this a delightful way to spend an afternoon. Open the same hours as the Visitor Center.

Buy a great gift and support MTRP! The Visitor and Interpretive Center has a gift shop specializing in nature-oriented educational items. Field guides, tee-shirts, walking sticks, and Kumeyaay crafts are just some of the great items available. Unique baskets and pottery are made by local Kumeyaay Indians using the same techniques applied for hundreds of years. The Gift Shop is open the same hours as the Visitor Center.

Be a *Friend* and support MTRP — Friends of Mission Trails and Friends of Lake Murray are two organizations with goals that benefit the Park today and into the future. Mission Trails Regional Park Foundation provides opportunities for individuals, businesses, community organizations and foundations to support a variety of programs and projects within the Park. Besides general support, special donations may be made to such things as the library, trail maintenance, tree and habitat maintenance and the Park's educational programs. Friends of Lake Murray sponsor a variety of projects to enhance the environment and provide visitor amenities at the Lake.

Call (619) 582-7800 for more information on donor opportunities, including memorial gifts, planned giving and bequests.

Disabled access — Park guests in wheelchairs will find the Visitor Center a delight. Not only are the exhibits and video programs inside the Center accessible, but there is a wide, gradually inclined walkway through the native plant garden adjacent to the Center. Be sure to ask for an interpretive brochure to help instruct your self-guided tour. Some of the easier trails may also be do-able in a wheelchair—such as the Father Junipero Serra Trail in the Mission Gorge Area and the paved path around Lake Murray. At Old Mission Dam there is a great viewing platform for the disabled overlooking the historic site. For information on other opportunities for disabled visitors, or to request a special program, contact Visitor Center staff, (619) 668-3278 or by e-mail mtrp@mtrp.org.

Campfire programs — Weather permitting, Park staff and special guests such as biologists, geologists and experts on Indian lore offer talks around a campfire on a variety of topics. Dates and times vary. Park in the campground day-use lot and meet at the campground amphitheater. Dress warmly and bring a flashlight. Campfire programs are canceled if it rains. For more information, call (619) 668-2748, or check the monthly events calendar at *www.mtrp.org*.

Public art and sculptures on view — Handcrafted art complements the natural beauty and history of Mission Trails. Surprisingly not all the breathtaking discoveries one can make within this open space jewel were crafted by Mother Nature. Take the time to check out several hand-made works of art when you visit. Sculptures in and around the Visitor and Interpretive Center are easy to find. As you walk up the winding path to the Center entrance you can't miss (but look closely or you'll miss one or two well-camouflaged ones!) the bronze life-like animal sculptures perched on rocks nearby. Find your way to the outside amphitheater and see a few more. Robert Berry a local self-taught sculptor created the animals, all replicas of ones found within the Park.

Just inside the entrance to the Center itself, turn to your right and meander among the red rock columns and even sit among them as you contemplate the emerging faces of Kumeyaay Indians—whose culture dates back thousands of years within this region. Sculptors T.J. Dixon and James Nelson invite visitors to consider, not only the physical beauty all around them in the Park, but also the rich history that preceded us here.

Requiring a little more effort to experience, but well worth it, is the public art known as "Water Marks," located at Deerfield Circle just off Mission Gorge Road. Artists Lynn Susholtz and Aida Mancillas used local stone, mosaic tiles, cast bronze sculptures of leaves, and carved animal footprints to create an abstract portrait of the San Diego River. This stunning piece, featured recently on the cover of Westways Magazine, echoes the topography of the Park while blending in with the surrounding landscape. Text that accompanies the sculpture is written in several languages, including that spoken by the Kumeyaay people, and invites the viewer to explore further.

"Was that a puddy-cat I saw?" — Yes, indeed, that was a real live cat sleeping in one of the comfy chairs in the Visitor Center or strolling by you in the exhibit area. This soft tortoise-shell female's name is "Kwaay Paay." She was rescued from an animal shelter to help keep the mice at bay inside the Center (remember you <u>are</u> in the heart of an animal-rich preserve after all). And she's doing a great job, thank you very much!

Her predecessor, "Fortuna," was the stuff of legends. Just when the staff was becoming concerned with a growing mouse problem in the newly constructed Center,

"Fortuna," a scrawny orange tabby appeared. The story goes that he was chased in by a very hungry coyote, just as he was using up the seventh of his nine lives. (More likely he was looking for some tasty leftovers at one of the opening events.) In any case, he lived out the remainder of his days adored, petted and pampered in the Visitor Center holding up his end of the bargain as a great mouser.

About the author:

Pamela Crooks is a writer, publisher and community volunteer. Local topics of historical and cultural interest are her specialty. San Diego's Mission Trails Regional Park is her second guidebook project. Published three years ago, **Discover Balboa Park: A Complete Guide to America's Greatest Urban Park** has sold out. A new edition is currently in development, as is a children's book about the famed San Diego horticulturist Kate Sessions. The author was first introduced to Mission Trails Regional Park when she and husband, Ted, moved to San Diego in 1976. Over the years they and their three sons have enjoyed hiking, birding, biking and school field trips in the Park. One of Pam's favorite places is the grinding rocks by the San Diego River where as one Trail Guide put it, "you can feel the presence of the Kumeyaay who once lived here."

About the contributors:

A native San Diegan, **Ruth C. Alter** holds B.A. and M.A. degrees in Anthropology from San Diego State University. She specializes in the interpretation of archaeological and historical subjects, as well as cultural resource management. Ms. Alter is the author of The Painted Rocks, a children's book focusing on the Piedras Pintadas site in Rancho Bernardo, and was the creative consultant for "*Stewardship through the Ages*," a film documenting the history of Mission Trails Regional Park. She is also the author of many environmental documents including the Cultural Resources Preservation Element for the City of Colton and the Historic Ordinance for the City of Murrieta.

Clark Rasmussen spent his youth in the northwest corner of Washington state in Bellingham and Lummi Island. Under the tutelage of his father and grandfather, both ardent outdoorsmen, Clark became immersed early on in nature and fitness. After a bad bicycle accident in 1997, he returned to hiking for rehabilitation at MTRP. Clark is a retired corporate pilot, an accomplished pianist, a patented inventor and active volunteer at the MTRP Visitor Center.

Sue Carlton Sifton, illustrator, is a graduate of San Diego State University's Fine Arts Department. Sue also spent much time in higher level biology courses while a student there. She's a devoted fan of Mission Trails Regional Park, knows a great deal about the flora and fauna from personal experience and wants others to enjoy the Park as she and her husband Ray, daughter Sarah, and son Ryan frequently do. Although Sue makes her living as a sculptor, she spent years developing her skills as a Nature illustrator.

INDEX

Acknowledgments

This guidebook has been a joy to work on! Foundation board members Gary Krueger and Don Steele championed the idea of a guidebook for the Park and shepherded the project through from beginning to end with the help of Barry Collins.

Archaeologist Ruth Alter's prior research and writing on the Park's early history enhanced Chapter 2. Further information about the last 40 years' history was shared with me in interviews with Pauline des Granges, Dorothy Leonard, Nancy Acevedo, Dick Brown and Jim Ellis. Barbara Anderson gave me background and current user-info for Lake Murray.

David Benedict, Center Director, and Roland Roberge, Foundation Administrative Assistant, helped set up interviews, find phone numbers, and delve into old newsletters and photographs at the state-of-the-art Visitor Center. Park Ranger Sue Pelley shared resources from a 30-hour training course every volunteer Trail Guide must complete. Sue also let me tag along on two great school field trips in the fall. Paul Kilburg, former Senior Park Ranger, shared his love and knowledge of Mission Trails that dates back to his childhood.

Park Rangers Rick Thompson, Mel Naidas, Casey Smith, and Luanne Barrett took time to educate me on their areas of expertise. Valuable hours were spent with Ranger Paul Seiley learning about native plants. Marla Gilmore, Campground Director, shared historical info on Kumeyaay Lake while Grounds Maintenance Worker Tom Folk detailed his first encounter with a vernal pool.

One spring Saturday morning I was privileged to attend a hands-on session with Trail Guide trainees. As the trainees demonstrated their knowledge giving plant talks and leading a trail walk, long-time docents like Bill Howell and George Varga confirmed or gently corrected their information. Bill's wealth of knowledge on the geology, flora and fauna of Mission Trails is astounding. His writings in Foundation newsletters and in the training manual were entertaining reading as well as educational.

It took me almost a year and four seasons before I felt I had a good handle on the depth and breadth of Mission Trails Regional Park. My faithful companions on most of the trails I hiked were either my husband, Ted, or our friend Steve Epstein. My son, Charles, also took photographs for me during one very wet hike in Oak Canyon. But I really didn't get to know the trails until I came under the tutelage of volunteer Clark Rasmussen, who donated many hours out in the Park fact-checking and correcting my hiking information.

Finally, the book design by Laurie Berg, illustrations by Sue Sifton and photography by many different people greatly enhanced the final product. All who worked on the book hope that by sharing this information more people will come to appreciate and enjoy the Park and help preserve it for future generations. Mission Trails Regional Park is awesome. My humble thanks to the many dedicated elected officials, public employees and community volunteers who have made it possible.

The Author

Resources

Printed Media:

Alden, Peter *National Audubon Society Field Guide to California*
Chanticleer Press, 1998

Alter, Ruth   Historical background/story treatment for *"Stewardship through the Ages"* Prepared for Mission Trails Regional Park Foundation, 2000

Belzer, Thomas J. *Roadside Plants of Southern California*
Mountain Press Publishing Co., 1984

Dale, Nancy *Flowering Plants of the Santa Monica Mountains*
California Native Plant Society, Santa Monica Chapter, 1999

Fisher, Chris C. and Clarke, Herbert *Birds of San Diego*

Lee, Melicent H. *Indians of the Oaks*, New Edition, Acoma books, 1978

Neugent, Sean, *"Visitor Center Interpretive Trail: Self-Guided Hike,"* pamphlet
City of San Diego Park & Recreation Department, 2001

Schad, Jerry and Copp, Nelson *Cycling San Diego: Revised Expanded Edition*
Centra Publications, 1996

Schad, Jerry *Afoot and Afield in San Diego, Third Edition* Wilderness Press, 1998

Sunbelt Natural History Map Series, *"Mission Trails Regional Park Trail Map"*
Sunbelt Publications, 2000

"Flowering Plants of Mission Trails Regional Park," pamphlet,
Mission Trails Regional Park Foundation, 2003

"Mission Trails Plant Identification Walk," pamphlet City of San Diego Park &
Recreation Department with MTRP Foundation, Inc.

"Mission Trails Regional Park News," quarterly newsletters
Mission Trails Regional Park Foundation, Inc., Vol. 1-14, 1990-2003

*"Multiple Species Conservation Program/ City of San Diego/ MSCP Subarea
Plan"* (Plan prepared by the City San Diego Community and Economic
Development Dept.) March 1997

*"Natural Community Conservation Planning 1991-1998: A Partnership for
Conservation,"* (A report funded by a grant from the National Fish and
Wildlife Foundation.), March 1999

"The Birds of Mission Trails Regional Park," pamphlet
City of San Diego Park & Recreation Department, 2003

"Trail Guide Training Manual," as maintained by the Park staff
(Binder used in training, includes contributions by Archaeologist Ruth
Alter, Writer Bill White, Naturalist Bill Howell, Geologist Shannon Dunn,
etc.), courtesy of Park Ranger Sue Pelley.

"San Diego Region's Diversity of Life," pamphlet Border XXI Natural Resources
Subcommittee, 2001

Video:

Holtzman, Jim, Writer/Producer **"Stewardship through the Ages"**
Broadcast Images for Mission Trails Regional Park Foundation, Inc., 2000

Web Sites:
The sites listed throughout the book were referred to again and again, and proved to be valuable sources of information for this project.

Additional Resources:
Resource Library, MTRP Visitor & Interpretive Center
San Diego County Library
San Diego Historical Society Archives & Web site, www.sandiegohistory.org
Junipero Serra Museum & San Diego Presidio Site
Mission San Diego de Alcala
Friends of Lake Murray
Mission Times Courier
Explore!

Photo Credits:
Front cover (counterclockwise): Mountaintop trail, Aaron Spears; Old Mission Dam in Fall, Charles Crooks; Visitor & Interpretive Center, Charles Crooks; Rock climber, Brent Jones; "Buzz off," Julie Warner.

Back cover: Spring in the Grasslands, Charles Crooks

Inside photographs:
First page (clockwise): Cactus flower, Travis Thomas; Photographer in Oak Canyon, Clarke Powell; Beetle on poppy, Weldon S. Thomson; Early morning on Lake Murray, Mary Ann Robinson.

Second page (top to bottom): Reflections of Fall, Edward C. Stalder; Bike ride at twilight, Brent Jones; Butterfly in the Grasslands, Tiffan Aptaker.

Third page: Prickly pear cactus bud, Travis Thomas; Stones in the river, Jason Schneider.

Fourth page: Red bush monkeyflower, Mike Hurlburt; Racoon tracks, Jeff Marshall.

Fifth page: Canyon wildflowers, Sandra Jeffers.

Sixth page (top to bottom): California lilacs, Ann Walker; MTRP resident, Mary Ann Robinson; Kwaay Paay after a storm, Rick Wiley.

Seventh page clockwise): Two species atop North Fortuna, Howard E. Maltz; Native grasses, Charles Crooks; River Camp, Sue Griffith; Cactus in full bloom, A.L. Edgar.

Eighth page (clockwise): Swamp fog on Kumeyaay Lake, Rick Wiley; Spider web in fall, Ann Walker; MTRP after rain, Rick Wiley; Geese at Lake Murray, Frank Phillips; Rattlesnake den, courtesy of MTRP staff.

🏃 25 Recommended Hikes in MTRP

Hiking Categories
1 = Easy, mostly level or gradual incline
2 = Okay for beginners in good physical condition
3 = Moderate, may require climbing over rocks and/or fairly steep incline
4 = Difficult, for hikers/bikers with good stamina, involves extended climbs
5 = Very challenging, for experienced hikers/bikers in excellent physical condition only

**Note: To hike "Level 4" or "Level 5" trails,
always wear hiking shoes with very good tread!!**

	Category	*Distance in Miles*
West Fortuna		
• Fortuna Saddle *from Visitor Center*	5	2.7 one way
• Fortuna Saddle *from Clairemont Mesa Blvd.*	4	1.8
• Suycott Wash / S. Fortuna Mtn. *(from "the Y")*	5	1.2+
• North/S. Fortuna Mtn. Loop *(from "the Saddle")*	5	4.1+
• Rim Trail Loop *(from CM Blvd.)*	3-4	3.1 roundtrip
• Quarry Loop Trail *(from CM Blvd.)*	2	2.1 roundtrip
• Shepherd Pond *(from CM Blvd.)*	3	2.3
East Fortuna		
• Grasslands Loop	1	1.2 roundtrip
• N. Fortuna *via Grasslands Crossing*	5	3.0
• Fortuna Saddle *from Mast Blvd.*	5	2.4
• Kumeyaay Lake Trail	1	1.0
• Fortuna Mountains Loop *(from Grasslands Xing)*	5	7.1 roundtrip
Mission Gorge Region		
• Visitor Center Loop	2	1.4 roundtrip
• Father Junipero Serra Trail	1	1.8
• Oak Grove Loop trail	1	1.0 roundtrip
• Oak Canyon Trail	3	1.7
• Climbers Loop Trail	5	1.0 roundtrip
• BMX Loop (from Visitor Ctr.)	2	1.1 roundtrip
• Kwaay Paay (from Old Mission Dam)	5	1.0
Cowles Mountain		
• Cowles Mtn. from Golfcrest & Navajo	5	1.5
• Cowles Mtn. from Barker Way (via service rd.)	4	1.6
• Cowles Mtn. from Big Rock Park in Santee	5	2.5
• Cowles Mtn. from Mesa Road in Santee	5	2.1
• Cowles Mtn. Summit to Pyles Peak	5	1.5+
Lake Murray Region		
• Lake Murray Hiking/Biking Path	1	3.2